Help! I'm a parent

Dr. Bruce Narramore

Illustrated by Diane Head

ZONDERVAN
PUBLISHING HOUSE
OF THE ZONDERVAN CORPORATION
GRAND RAPIDS, MICHIGAN 49506

Second printing   September 1972
Third printing   1973

ACKNOWLEDGMENTS

I used to think acknowledgments by authors were only routine,
superficial tributes to the author's friends. Now I feel very different about it. My wife, Kathy, played a key role in developing this
book. We spent many hours discussing child-rearing practices and
learning from our own mistakes. After the manuscript was written,
Kathy moved carefully between the roles of a supportive, encouraging wife and a harsh critic. Her contributions added immeasurably
to the quality of this book.

My secretary, Mrs. Diane Head, also made terrific contributions.
She has an amazing knack to take my illegible scribblings and turn
them into a beautifully typed manuscript ready for the next go-
round of editing.

While I can't honestly make the trite statement, "without them
this book may never have been written," I can gratefully say that
without them it could not have been written well!

DEDICATION

A story is told of a young child psychologist who started his practice with four theories and no children. Some years later he had four children and no theories! I dedicate this book to

DICKIE *and* DEBBIE

who have transformed at least two of my theories from abstract generalizations to workable techniques for raising children. I pray that our home will give them the fertile soil needed to unfold the unique personalities God has stored up in their genes.

CONTENTS

PART 1

Biblical and Psychological Foundations of Child Rearing

With so many conflicting ideas on child rearing, today's parent needs a firm foundation. All efforts at child discipline should be grounded in objective truth. Parents shouldn't vacillate with each new trend or theory. Part 1 of this book explains the groundwork for our approach to child rearing. By drawing on both biblical and psychological truth, a solid basis for rearing children is established. The Bible gives a great foundation for the parent-child relation. It also serves as a corrective force to balance the whims of current psychological theory. By combining the practical insights of modern psychology with the lasting truths of the Bible, we have a solid and balanced approach to the problems of the modern parent. The basic insights of Part 1 will later be followed by specific techniques for guiding your child's behavior.

Chapter 1

PARENT TO PARENT

"I just don't know what to do with our kids!" complained a frustrated mother. "Every day is another hassle. From morning to night something is always going wrong. We have tried everything, but nothing seems to work!"

Most of us can sympathize with this. We have all had trying times with children. In some families a healthy peace is interrupted only occasionally by a temper tantrum, a crying spell, or disobedience. This is to be expected. But other homes are in turmoil from dawn to dusk. The struggle begins with mother's morning wake-up call. Pulling the covers over his head Johnny murmurs, "O.K. In a few minutes." Later mother warns, "You've got to get up or you'll be late for school!" When there is still no response mother finally shouts, "Johnny! Get out of bed this minute!" Johnny slowly crawls out of bed. Now the scene changes to the bathroom. Since Johnny is slow as usual, mother calls, "Hurry up and get out of the bath — your sister is waiting!" After several more naggings and very little response from Johnny, we finally make it to the kitchen. But Johnny doesn't want to eat. He dawdles while coming to the table — then plays with his food. Finally it's 8:15. The school bus will be arriving any second. Frantically packing the children's lunches, mother brings Johnny his coat and books, and shoves him out the door — his breakfast still on the table. Breathing a sigh of relief, mother pours herself another cup of coffee and prepares for the rest of her daily duties.

Encounters like this are happening to thousands daily. Parents and children are frustrated, but no one knows how to improve the state of confusion. These conflicts are "normal." Nevertheless, they rob families of rich opportunities for pleasure and unity. Parenthood becomes frustrating and childhood an unhappy time. As these experiences pile up, children move into set patterns of maladjustment. These habit patterns are the seeds to later problems in life. After falling into the habit of getting his way through negative means, a child finds it difficult to change. He carries these same behaviors to school. When he becomes an adult, they show up day after day. They are relived in the home and at the office. These apparently "normal" childhood frustrations become the foundation of adult emotional problems. But this doesn't have to happen. With understanding parental planning, *they can be overcome!*

Encounters between parent and child also stir up clashes in marriage. Struggling with constant bickering, a wife directs hostility to her husband. She bombards him with comments like "You are so thoughtless and selfish"; "You never help with the kids"; or "How do you expect me to take care of *these kids* and get your dinner on time?" Soon father is angry. He hides behind the newspaper or tries to settle the whole affair by telling everyone to shut up and mind his own business!

Scenes like this pose an interesting question. *Why is it that well-meaning, loving parents have children who are uncooperative and maladjusted?* My counseling experience with hundreds of parents has shown that in many families neither the parents nor the child have deep emotional disturbances. Instead, parents as well as children have learned maladaptive patterns of reacting to other family members. Children have built up ingenious ways of manipulating mom and dad, and parents have failed to learn positive, constructive ways of relating to their children's misbehavior.

Our society demands seventeen years of education before certifying a person to teach in the public schools. Medical doctors must have twenty years of schooling. Carpenters and plumbers go through several years of apprenticeship and training before reaching full efficiency in their fields. *But for the work of rearing a child from the crib, we give absolutely no formal training!* Perhaps this is because conception, pregnancy, and childbirth are all natural body functions which move along without any special training. We assume (if we think about it at all) that child rearing "just comes naturally." But it has become glaringly apparent that this is not so. The daily conflicts in every home, the staggering fact of emotional disturbance and mental illness, and the increasing social and behavioral problems of our society all point to the failure of present approaches to child training. In the United States it is estimated that one in twelve people will spend some time in a mental hospital. Countless others are in need of less drastic forms of treatment for emotional disturbances and adjustment problems.

The quality of family life experienced by children affects much more than their emotional adjustment. It seriously influences their spiritual development. This, of course, is an eternal consideration. I once asked a woman to describe her father. She replied, "He is loving, kind, just, and a fine gentleman . . . but I feel he is so distant." Some weeks later I asked her to tell me about God. She replied, "He is loving, kind, just, and omnipotent . . . but He seems so distant." She used almost the exact words in describing God and her own father! This is not uncommon.

A child's image of God is strongly influenced by his relations with his parents. Since God is an immaterial Person

located in a seemingly distant heaven He is hard for a child
to comprehend. Foreseeing this problem, God created the
family structure to teach us about His nature. We live in a
natural, physical world. There is also a spiritual world. To
bridge the gap between the two, God uses concepts from our
physical world to teach truths from the spiritual realm. He
uses light (John 8:12)[1] to represent the True Light. He uses
the vine (John 15:1, 2)[2] to represent the True Vine. And He
uses a father (Hebrews 12:7-10)[3] to represent the True
Father. As a child grows he learns about the love and justice
of his earthly father. When he is told about God he begins
to understand. His unconscious reasoning goes something
like this: "God, whom I have not seen, is a heavenly Father.
He must be like my father. Now I can understand what God
is like."

The carry-over from earthly to heavenly Father is clearly
shown in Matthew 7:11 where Christ said, "If ye then being
evil, know how to give good gifts unto your children, how
much more shall your Father which is in heaven give good
things to them that ask him?" This passage indicates that a
child can expect to see the virtues of his parents magnified
in his heavenly Father. Where few of these virtues exists, it
is hard to build up a positive image of God.

[1] John 8:12, "Then spake Jesus unto them, saying, I am the light of the
world: he that followeth me shall not walk in darkness, but shall have the
light of life."

[2] John 15:1, 2, "I am the true vine, and my Father is the husbandman.
Every branch in me that beareth not fruit he taketh away: and every branch
that beareth fruit, he purgeth it, that it may bring forth more fruit."

[3] Hebrews 12:7-10 (Amplified Bible), "You must submit to and endure
[correction] for discipline. God is dealing with you as with sons; for what
son is there whom his father does not [thus] train and correct and discipline? Now if you are exempt from correction and left without discipline
in which all [of God's children] share, then you are illegitimate offspring
and not true sons [at all]. Moreover, we have had earthly fathers who
disciplined us and we yielded [to them] and respected [them for training
us]. Shall we not much more cheerfully submit to the Father of spirits
and so [truly] live?"

Loving and mature parents make it easy for children to understand God's character. But anxious, inconsistent, or domineering parents instill a poor father-image. Children of these parents may see God as distant, unconcerned, punitive, or weak. The exact image depends on the attributes of his earthly parents.

The teenage daughter of a harsh, critical minister once came to me for counseling. She was severely depressed. In her suffering she tried to commit suicide to end her misery. While talking about her relation to God, she said with great anger, "Don't give me that ―― ――― about 'God is love'! If He were love, I would see it in my father!" This reaction and others like it are rehearsed daily in counseling offices around the world. Many people look for God, but their vision is clouded by an earthly parent.

A story is told of a father who put his young son on a table top and said, "Jump to daddy." When the boy jumped, his father stepped aside and let him fall to the floor. "That will teach you never to trust anyone!" the father said cynically. This parental action is extreme. But children often learn that they cannot trust. We spank a child in anger and tell him, "This is for your good," rather than admitting, "This makes me feel better." We make a promise and fail to keep it. Through this, our children are gradually learning not to trust. When they become Christians they want to trust God. But somehow it is hard. They have trusted many times and have been let down. Now their feelings whisper, "Be careful. You can't depend on Him. You may be used, or you may be hurt."

My experience in counseling neurotic adults has invariably shown that their image of God has been colored by negative experiences with parents, God's representatives on earth. This is not to say that biblical teachings on God's character fail to influence our spiritual relationships. They certainly

do. *But negative emotional reactions stemming from child-*
hood interfere with our ability to apply biblical knowledge.
Think of your own Christian experience. Haven't you sometimes feared a vengeful God, or felt He didn't understand?
Have you had difficulty believing God's will was best for
you? Have you resented God's direction or discipline? Most
of these feelings are emotional hangovers from childhood
experiences.

In a real sense God has given us a divine opportunity to
shape our children's lives for time and for eternity. It is
beautiful to realize we can actually teach our children the
love and character of God. It is awesome to know that our
own hang-ups can drive wedges between our precious children and God, the Creator of the universe.

As a psychologist and parent I am vitally concerned with
these family problems. I had four years of professional experience in child-guidance clinics before my first child was
born. It didn't take long to realize that profound psychological statements such as "He is an insecure child"; "He is suffering from hyperactivity"; or "He is afraid of experiencing
parental rejection" didn't really describe the problems I and
other parents were facing at home! Neither did counsel such
as "Show her more love"; "Be consistent"; or "Build up his
ego" do much to change the daily behavior of the average
child.

Since my wife and I were college graduates, and I had a
Ph.D., we naturally assumed we were ready for parenthood.
But we were surprised! Our kids had the same problems
as those across the street. We found ourselves plagued by
temper tantrums, crying spells, hostile outbursts and a variety
of other actions not altogether becoming to children of a
practicing psychologist! As Christians, we wanted to give
our children a good start in life. But we had to make a
decision. Were we going to sit back and worry or get down

to business and find some solid, workable answer? This book is the result of that search.

But no book can make us into "instant parents." This is a gradual process. Effective parenthood takes *knowledge* of proper parental responses. It takes *insight* into the parent-child relationship. And it takes *practice* in carrying out correct reactions. To help you in this process a manual for parents has been developed. This manual, *A Guide to Child Rearing,* is coordinated with *Help! I'm a Parent! A Guide to Child Rearing* helps you understand your child and gives specific steps in teaching new behaviors. This Guide is the key to *Help! I'm a Parent!* By carrying out the assignments in the Guide you will soon see positive growth in your child's behavior.

Chapter 2

THE NATURE OF CHILDHOOD

During a Wednesday morning mother's club, Annette was recounting a recent frustration. "I told my boy he was acting just like a two-year-old," she blurted out. "How old is he?" my wife asked. "Two!" Annette replied, somewhat embarrassed! She was baffled because her child was acting like a normal two-year-old! This is common. We usually expect our children to be more mature than their developmental level. We don't like it when they "act their age." [1]

To rear children properly we must have a clear concept of the nature of childhood. We must know how our children see their world. We must recognize their wants, their goals, their needs, and their fears. This chapter will acquaint you with your child's emotional needs. It will disclose some of the "hidden reasons" for your child's behavior. Also, it will provide help in understanding his "private world."

---

[1] The most thorough studies on child development were done by Dr. Arnold Gesell at Yale University. Hundreds of children were studied for several years to find the average ages at which they showed various specific physical, mental, and emotional characteristics. Here are three books which give these age expectancies from birth to sixteen years of age.

Arnold Gesell et. al. *The First Five Years of Life,* N.Y.: Harper Brothers Publishers, 1940.

Arnold Gesell and Frances Ilg, *The Child From Five to Ten,* N.Y.: Harper Brothers Publishers, 1946.

Arnold Gesell, Frances Ilg, and Louise Bates Ames, *Youth: The Years From Ten to Sixteen,* N.Y.: Harper Brothers Publishers, 1956.

CONFIDENCE AND POWER

Lying in a crib, a newborn infant is totally dependent. Without others, he will die. He is unable to care for himself and is at the mercy of his environment. Soon baby finds that his cries bring parents running. When he is hungry, he cries. When he is wet, he cries. This is his first success in controlling a big, powerful world.

A child's world is a bewildering place. He is surrounded by powerful adults and children who are competing for the attention he desires. He is weak and under the domination of others. Each time he has a need he develops a feeling of tension. To overcome this tension he must find ways of gaining control over his world. He must get others to supply his needs. He must build his confidence and gain a sense of power. By controlling his surroundings, he will feel safe and secure. *Learning to control his world is a child's first goal.* This control is of two types. There is a positive need for confidence and a negative drive for power. Children must develop a sense of confidence to become emotionally healthy. But an unchecked drive for power can turn a child into a demanding tyrant.

Mary had just been tucked in bed by mother. As Mr. and Mrs. Turner were making themselves comfortable in the living room, Mary quietly tip-toed down the hall. "I want to kiss daddy good night," she said with a winsome smile. "Daddy already told you good night, Mary. Now back to bed!" replied Mrs. Turner. Minutes later Mary called again, "Mommy, I need a drink of water." "You just had one!" Mrs. Turner called back, her voice rising. "Now go to sleep!" Soon Mary called again, "Mommy, I have to go to the bathroom." "All right!" Mrs. Turner called impatiently, "but hurry back to bed." "But, mommy, I can't get my pajamas off." "O.K. I'm coming!" yelled Mrs. Turner as she headed down the hall with anger in her eyes!

Mary and her mother were in a power struggle. Mrs. Turner was trying to force her child to stay in bed. Mary was determined to get out again. When Mary was sent to bed, mother was in control. To reverse that arrangement, Mary had to fight to win her way. By calling until Mrs. Turner finally gave in, Mary won control for a while. She got the attention she wanted, proved she didn't have to go to bed, and received the added enjoyment of upsetting her mother! Her refusal to go to sleep was caused by her search for power and control.

The search for a sense of confidence and control may also lead to desired behavior. Running into the house after school, Susie yells excitedly, "Mother, see what I made today?" She is proud of her achievement and is looking for praise that will build her confidence.

Young boys often search for confidence through imitating their dad's behavior. "See how strong I am!" says three-year-old Freddie as he struggles in the house with a watermelon, half his size. Father exclaims, worriedly: "Look out! You'll drop it. It's too heavy!" Out of concern over the watermelon, he is telling Freddie he is weak and small. How much better to quickly but gently take the melon and say, "Thanks, son. You're such a big help!" This approach would save both the watermelon and Freddie's sense of confidence.

A desire for confidence is a God-given need. We all want to feel confident and adequate. A feeling of confidence is one sign of emotional maturity. It is that inner peace that comes with a good feeling about our abilities. We should try to build up these positive feelings in our children.

A search for confidence and power becomes bad only when it leads to conflicts and struggles for power. Some people can never feel secure unless they are in control. This is emotionally unhealthy, but all children have a little of this. They think they must be in command to feel secure. They

test every rule to gain a feeling of power. They try to break rules to prove their strength. Impulsively they desire complete control. But at a deeper level, children want controls. When limits are not enforced, they become insecure. They feel anxious when they succeed in throwing off parental boundaries. When we give in to childish demands and manipulations for power, we do not help. This only reinforces negative behavior and leads to further problems.

LOVE AND ATTENTION

It was 6:00 p.m. and Mr. Williams had just returned from work. Settling into an easy chair, he opened the evening paper. About that time five-year-old Joey pushed the paper aside and said, "Daddy, will you play with me?" "Not now, son. I just got home and I'm very tired," replied Mr. Williams, continuing to read. Soon Joey was back. "Daddy, will you play with me now?" "Not yet, Joey. I'm still reading." "But, dad, I want you to see my new game!" "Later, son! I'm busy now." answered Mr. Williams, a little frustrated. After a few minutes of peace, Joey came again. "You never play with me!" he accused. Feeling somewhat guilty and knowing he would have no peace until Joey was satisfied, Mr. Williams reluctantly went to see his son's new game. After a few minutes of play, Joey was satisfied and dad was able to return to his paper.

This everyday incident illustrates two other goals of child behavior. Joey was looking for love and attention. Seeing dad behind the newspaper made him feel left out. He was out of dad's attention. This made him feel like a second-rate citizen. *This search for a feeling of love and attention is probably the most important explanation of your child's behavior.* When positive actions fail to meet their needs, children turn to misbehavior.

Mrs. Cox spent a busy morning in the kitchen. Being so involved, she had little time for Susie. Deciding to check on her two-year-old, Mrs. Cox found her proudly displaying artistic creations on the bedroom wall! "What have you done?" scolded Mrs. Cox. "You know better than that!" And surely Susie did. But she wanted her mother's attention. Being a good, quiet child wouldn't work. If Susie minded her own business mother might spend all day in the kitchen. The only way to draw mother's attention was to misbehave.

We all want love and affection. This is a God-given need. Without a feeling of companionship life is dull, lonely, and depressing. With it, life becomes an exciting adventure. One

of the greatest joys in life is the continued opportunity to express parental love.

Unfortunately, some children fail to distinguish between love and attention. Love is a constructive need. But an undue search for attention isn't good. Some children think they must be the center of attention in order to be loved. If they are not getting attention, they feel alone and rejected. This is an unrealistic and childish misperception. Giving in to all demands for attention leads to self-centeredness and spoiled behavior. Children become our masters, and we become their slaves. They refuse to give us a moment of peace. They play on our sense of responsibility to rule our lives. In short, they are tyrants in small bodies!

Carolyn was this type of girl. Her constant cry was, "Mommy, I need you," or "Mommy, come play." Mrs. Evans couldn't begin a chore without her pleading interruptions. Carolyn had her mother on a string. When she pulled, mother came running. This is an unfortunate arrangement.

When children continue their attention-getting behavior we have three alternatives. *We can drop everything each time they call.* This meets the child's demands, gives a temporary peace, and relieves our guilt for being "rejecting parents." But it doesn't solve the problems.

Another way of managing this irritating search for attention is to *ignore it completely.* By totally refusing to listen, we withdraw the rewards of attention. Seeing that continual interruptions do not get more attention, Carolyn would soon stop her undesirable behavior. But this solution poses a problem. Maybe Carolyn's need for love is genuine. Maybe she is lonely and afraid. Perhaps she really needs her mother's constant approval. To ignore her under these circumstances would be cruel! We should never simply ignore our children's desires for attention.

Repeated attention-getting behavior is telling us one of two things. Either our children have unmet needs for love, or they are trying to control us. The third solution is based on these ideas. To be sure we are meeting our children's needs for love, we should evaluate our family relationships. Are we communicating well? Do we take time to play our children's games? Do they really know we think they are very important to us? If so, we can tell them something like this, "Carolyn, you know how much mommy loves you. We have had some good times today. Now mother has some work to do. If you call again I will not come and I will not answer. You can play with your toys and mommy will do her work. Later we can play some more." In doing this, you have accomplished two things. *You assured your child of your love, but you refused to let her rule your day.* This is good for both mother and child. To teach children a proper view of love, we must meet their genuine emotional needs but refuse to be manipulated by unrealistic demands for attention.

WORTHINESS AND PERFECTION

Another goal of child behavior is to find a sense of worthiness and value. Worthiness implies a moral judgment of being a "good child." In trying to meet this need, most children develop positive behavior patterns to meet the approval of parents and others. We should take care to acknowledge good behavior and build our children's sense of worthiness.

The mother of a newly adopted little girl recently complained of having great difficulty making her daughter behave. Finally she found a solution. She proudly reported, "I told her, 'God doesn't love you when you're naughty!'" "Just a minute," I replied. "Does God love *you* when *you* are naughty?" She got the point! She had manipulated her daughter into proper behavior by implying she was not a good person. She was teaching her daughter that she didn't deserve love when she acted that way. How terrible! The whole message of Christ is that God loves us just as we are. Children are keenly sensitive to such evaluations. They try to be good to merit approval and love. But when this fails, they develop a sense of unworthiness which may cause serious emotional problems.

Some children confuse a sense of worth with personal perfectionism. At the slightest indication of unacceptable behavior they are hurt. Sensing their parents' unrealistic expectations, they try to be above reproach. They become "model children" with no hint of negative emotions; they repress each tinge of anger and deny their sexual feelings. They try for excellent grades and their performanance is always superior. Fearing condemnation for any personal weakness, they are motivated to become "perfect angels." While this motivation leads to "desirable" behavior, it also causes feelings of depression and despair. Children need to know that they are judged as worthy and important just for who they are. The need for perfectionism to gain a sense of worth is psychologically unhealthy.

Now we have the six main goals of child behavior: (1) love, (2) attention, (3) confidence, (4) power, (5) worthiness, and (6) perfection. Feelings of love, confidence, and worth are healthy emotions. But when children don't experience positive feelings, they look for substitute fulfillments. Being the center of attention helps hide a sense of loneliness. Controlling others by the use of power covers the anxiety caused by a lack of confidence. Being perfect is a substitute for a healthy sense of worth. In this way attention, power, and perfectionism are counterfeit reactions. They are our children's misguided efforts to satisfy needs of love, confidence, and worth.

REVENGE

Something else happens when a child's emotional needs aren't met. A frustrated search for love, confidence, or worth causes further negative reactions. The child turns to two types of misbehavior. The first is anger or revenge. The second is a search for psychological safety.

Let's take the adopted child whose mother is repeatedly

telling her she is naughty and bad. This girl will soon learn she can never be good in her mother's eyes. After continually failing to win mother's approval, she becomes discouraged and angry — discouraged because she can never feel good about herself, and angry because mother has made her feel this way.

One of the best ways to retaliate against this type of moralistic mother is to become really a "bad" child. Developing behavior which hurts and dismays parents is a common method of gaining revenge. The rebellious son of a minister who had routinely neglected his family for Christian work came to me for counseling. During the interview he said, "Sometimes when I'm really drunk, I pick up a beer and say, 'Here's one for the deacons' board!'" Resenting the lack of attention from his father, he sought to retaliate by drunkenness. There was probably nothing that upset his father more. This, he thought correctly, was an effective way to get revenge!

One evening Robert was seeking attention by pestering his younger sister. His mother said, "Cut it out, or go to your room!" Not to lose the struggle, Robert got in one final taunt to his sister. True to her threat, mother sent Robert to his room. Soon a loud pounding was heard. Upon investigation, Mrs. Dickens found Robert had taken his toy hammer and purposely knocked a hole in his bedroom door! Mrs. Dickens had thought she had won the battle by sending Robert to bed. But he got in the final blow! This interaction shows three of the goals of child behavior. Robert was seeking attention by teasing his younger sister. When his mother became angry and threatened to send him to bed, she initiated a *power struggle* that Robert didn't intend to lose. When mother sent Robert to bed, he was losing the power struggle, and that made him angry. The hammer episode was *his way of retaliating* against his mother for frustrating his goals of attention and power. Nearly every conflict follows this same pattern. A need is frustrated, a power struggle develops, and retaliation follows.

A SEARCH FOR PSYCHOLOGICAL SAFETY

The other way of responding to frustration in meeting the goals of love, confidence, and worth is the use of a variety of defense mechanisms designed to insure psychological safety. When a child's efforts to find love and attention keep meeting with rejection, he finally stops trying and *withdraws* for fear of further hurt. Critical parents sometimes tear down a child's feeling of confidence and lead him to give up trying at all. By withdrawing from possible failure and rejection, he protects himself from further frustration of his emotional needs.

Other children develop what psychologists call *reaction formation*. Strong feelings of hostility and rebellion are condemned or forbidden by parents. Knowing he will feel guilty or rejected if he shows his true feelings, a child puts on an outward show of compliance and love. This covers the inner emotions of anger and resentment.

Susie was that type of girl. Every time she said, "I'm angry," or "I hate you!" her parents got a shocked look on their faces. Her father tried to squash the anger by retorting loudly, "Don't you talk to your father that way! Now you go to your room!" Susie's mother would say, "Susie! What an awful thing to say! Don't you know Christians shouldn't talk that way?" In different ways mother and dad were both saying, "You cannot be angry. That is wrong. We don't like you when you're mad."

So what did Susie do? Did her parents' condemnation and punishment resolve her hostile feelings? Of course not! They only made her more angry. But since Susie was afraid to be angry, she pressed the feelings into her unconscious mind. On the outside, she seemed pleasant and cooperative. But within she was seething with anger. Later in life this anger is likely to erupt toward her parents, or be turned on herself in the form of depression and guilt.

Other children try to insure psychological safety through *over-compensation*. Billy had a great lack of confidence. He was a small boy and couldn't make friends easily. Not wanting to think of himself as an outsider, Billy started to study diligently. Soon he was at the top of his class. Since he hadn't found social acceptance, he hoped to gain some stature through his grades. He was compensating for feelings of rejection by academic overachievement. This was Billy's attempt to insure his psychological safety and protect his self-esteem.

All children use some defense mechanism like withdrawal, reaction formation, and overcompensation. But when a child develops a strong pattern of these defenses, he may be trying to protect himself from the frustration of his needs for love, confidence, and worth. It is absolutely essential for parents of these children to become more sensitive to ways of meeting their emotional needs.

THE POWER STRUGGLE

Practically every clash between parent and child involves a struggle for power. In some way or other the child is saying, "I will show you who's boss." Most parents take up this challenge without realizing the results. They try to prove their authority to the child, only to find they never win.

Bobby's mother said, "Son, please pick up your toys before company comes." "No! I won't!" Bobby exclaimed, being in a bad mood. "Yes, you will!" Mrs. Hansen retorted. "You got them out; now pick them up!" "All right," said

Bobby reluctantly, as he put a couple of blocks away and disappeared. Finding the mess a few minutes later, Mrs. Hansen called angrily, "Bobby, you pick up these things immediately!" Soon the toys were gone and company arrived. Later that night Mrs. Hansen found the blocks dumped in the middle of Bobby's bedroom.

Here we have a struggle for power. Mrs. Hansen was determined to have Bobby pick up his blocks. Bobby was just as determined to prove he could do things his own way. He got a real sense of power by refusing to cooperate with mother.

How are we to cope with this play for power? The natural response for most of us is to fight power with power. Since we are larger, stronger, and smarter (we hope!), we assume we can withstand the attacks of children and maintain a position of authority. If a child disobeys, we can beat him into submission. If he fails to carry out some task, we can create an unpleasant consequence to punish him. If Johnny brings home three D's on his report card, we can withhold his allowance, reprimand him, remove his television privileges, or intervene in some other way.

But there are problems with the use of power. First of all, *it usually doesn't work!* A child has his own weapons. There is no way to make him do better in school. It is impossible to force a child to eat. As a matter of fact, the more you pressure a child to improve his grades or better his eating habits, the less likely he is to cooperate. Underachieving and not eating may be your child's way of gaining power or getting revenge. He knows these things annoy you. The more worried you are, the better he likes it. Every time you nag, coerce, scold, or punish, he thinks unconsciously, *Oh, boy! I'm winning now!* Try as you will, there are many things you can't force a child to do. Passive resistance is one of his greatest weapons. By failing, dawdling, or refusing to eat, *your child is showing you he will not be controlled.*

Any time a child involves us in a power struggle he has won control. Even though we force the right behavior from him, he has manipulated our feelings to the point of anger, fear, or frustration. To a child, this is victory. Whenever a child makes us lose our temper, *he* has won a victory.

Take undereating, for example. As soon as you say, "Johnny, you *must* finish your meat," Johnny has you where he wants you. He has drawn you into a state of frustration and is not about to help you out by finishing his meal. Let's say you threaten to spank him till he finally cleans his plate. Do you think you have won? Not at all! You've forced him to eat his food, all right. But he forced you into worry, nagging, frustration, and anger. Everyone loses in this arrangement.

Another limitation of parental power is its arbitrary nature. "Why do I have to?" a child inquires. "Because I said so!" father firmly retorts. Although the child may obey his father, the command has taught very little. The restriction was not meaningful to the child since its only purpose was "because daddy said so." *Although the child may learn obedience, he is not learning self-control.*

All this is not to say a parent shouldn't exert his authority. God has placed you in a position of responsibility and has given you the authority to go with it. The Bible clearly teaches that children are to obey their parents. Ephesians 6:1 says, "Children, obey your parents in the Lord: for this is right." Obviously you should not allow your child to play near a swimming pool when he is unable to swim. In a situation of potential danger you should pick up your child and remove him to a safe place. He may scream and cry. But if you are acting out of a realistic concern *with a totally calm attitude,* you are not in a power struggle. You exerted your God-given authority in a constructive way, but were not drawn into a power struggle. You could have argued with your child, threatened to spank him if he didn't move away, or grabbed him in anger and taken him to a safe place. In each of those reactions you would have been involved in a power struggle because of your attitude.

The problem with parental power comes when we use our authority at improper times and in improper ways. We often kid ourselves into thinking we are "doing what's best for our child" when we are actually demonstrating our own power, ventilating our own frustrations, or perpetuating some useless family tradition! Later we will discuss the authority and responsibility of parents in greater depth. The important point for now is to realize that when we attempt to force our children to obey, we usually raise our children's anger and complicate our problem. It is better to use other methods to win our child's cooperation.

DETECTING THE POWER STRUGGLE

It is impossible to train children correctly as long as we are involved in a power struggle. Struggles for power and effective child rearing just don't mix. If you want to restore peace to your home and effectively discipline your children, you must learn to recognize the power struggle and take steps to avoid it. The first hint of a power struggle is our attitude. Whenever we feel angry or frustrated, we are in a power struggle no matter what we do! Children read us like an open book. We think they don't know our feelings. But they can quickly sense our "hidden frustrations." Children are often more sensitive to the power struggle than parents are.

Tone of voice is another clue in detecting a power struggle. We often say in a loud voice, "Of course I'm not angry!" Although we convince ourselves of our pure motives and calm attitude, our voice gives us away. We are still involved in a struggle for power.

Our child's reactions are a third way of discovering the power struggle. When a child is stubborn or negativistic over a period of time, we must be involved in a struggle. "It takes two to tango!" If we were not involved in battle, his struggle for power would disappear.

A power struggle can become a well-established habit that is not easily broken. Our own fears, goals, frustration, guilt, and anger are tied to our behavior. These feelings make it difficult to learn new ways of responding to children. Part 4 on "Parents are People, Too" gives practical advice on handling negative emotions. For the time being, it is essential to start recognizing the power struggle and attempting to avoid it.

Chapter 3

DISCIPLINE'S DIVINE DESIGN

In 1971, *Look* magazine devoted an entire issue to "The American Family." Most of the articles stressed the failure of our current family structure and the need for new patterns of living. Alternatives such as communal living and short-term contract marriages were suggested as possible "improvements." Echoing the failure of the present system, one of the writers, Alvin Toffler, wrote as follows:

> My own hunch is that most people will try to go blindly through the motions of the traditional marriage, and try to keep the traditional family going, and they'll fail. And the consequence will be a subtle but very significant shift to much more temporary marital arrangements, an intensification of the present pattern of divorce and remarriage and divorce and remarriage to the point at which we accept the idea that marriages are not for life. I'm not endorsing it, but I think it's likely to be the case. [1]

In contrast to the many attacks on the "outdated" American family, the Bible has some very clear teachings. The family is not a short-term sociological phenomenon that has filled a temporary purpose and is now no longer needed. Instead, it is foundational to every culture. This chapter is designed to give a clear picture of the vital necessity of effective family living for the entire society. Without this basic institution we are sure to be plagued by increasing personal and social crises.

When God placed Adam and Eve on this planet, He established the family as the basic unit of society. This was

[1] "The American Family," *Look*, Volume 25, Number 2, January 26, 1971.

essential to His plan for the human race. God designed the family structure for some extremely vital reasons. *The first was to provide for the needs of every family member.* Eve was created because Adam was lonely. He needed a companion. In return for her companionship, Adam was to love Eve and supply her needs. When Cain and Abel entered the home, Adam and Eve were to provide their necessities. As parents, we have similar responsibilities. We are to meet the total needs of our children. These include the physical, the spiritual, and the emotional. The following biblical passages point up some of our responsibilities to children:

Spiritual needs: Deuteronomy 6:6, 7

> And these words, which I command thee this day, shall be in thine heart: And thou shalt *teach them diligently unto thy children,* and shalt talk of them when thou sittest in thine house, and when thou walkest by the way, and when thou liest down, and when thou risest up.

Physical needs: 2 Corinthians 12:14b

> For the children ought not to lay up for the parents, but the parents for the children.

Emotional needs: Titus 2:4

> That they may teach the young women to be sober, to love their husbands, *to love their children.*

Total needs: 1 Timothy 5:8

> But if any provide not for his own, and specially for those of his own house, he hath denied the faith and is worse than an infidel.

In creating the family, God also wanted to teach us about Himself. Wives are to learn of Christ's love for the Church through the loving example of their husbands. Men are to learn of Christ's faithfulness and love by living the "husband" role with their wives. Children are to learn of God's love and character through the witness of their parents. Every family relationship is designed to build up our understanding of the character of God.

A *third reason for establishing the family lies in a child's need for guidance.* We each enter life with great potential for good and evil. Although babies aren't consciously sinning creatures, they are born into this world under sin. They are bent to self-centeredness, rebelliousness, and evil. Psalm 51:5 says, "Behold, I was shapen in iniquity; and in sin did my mother conceive me." Proverbs 22:15 develops this idea further. It reads, "Foolishness is bound in the heart of a child; but the rod of correction shall drive it far from him." These verses are in great contrast to the statements of some who resist the biblical teaching that children are sinful. They insist that we are born good, or at least morally neutral. This opinion has a great bearing on our child rearing practices. If children are essentially neutral we can adopt a permissive attitude toward discipline. Much of the system of "progessive education" and "permissive" child rearing is based on this premise. In brief, the thought is this: "If children are basically good, they need little adult direction and discipline. Given sufficient love and a good environment, they will develop into mature, good citizens." Any parent who carefully considers his child's behavior has a hard time buying this modern notion. Even young children show a stubborn, selfish will which lies at the heart of sin. If man is so good, what happened to Adam and Eve? They lived in a perfect environment yet they fell into sin. They really couldn't blame their parents for their problems!

All this is not to say that a child's environment is not important. It certainly is. Proverbs says we must bring up our children properly if they are to maintain their faith as adults. There is a dual responsibility for the development of sinful behavior. Some lies with the child; [2] the rest lies

2 Proverbs 20:11, "Even a child is known by his doings, whether his work be pure, and whether it be right."

with the parents. [3] Both parent and child share the responsibility for the child's personal development.

Since children are born without knowledge and with a
bent to evil, it was necessary for God to provide a way of
training each new member of society. A child's old sinful
nature doesn't magically pass away. It must be controlled,
disciplined, and eventually yielded to the new influence of
the Holy Spirit. To accomplish this task, God gave kids
parents! There are a few biblical passages on the necessity
and responsibility for parental discipline!

> And now a word to you parents. Don't keep on scolding
> and nagging your children, making them angry and resent-
> ful. Rather, bring them up with the loving discipline the
> Lord Himself approves, with suggestions and godly advice.
>
> Ephesians 6:4 (*The Living Bible*)
>
> Withhold not correction from the child: for if thou beatest
> him with the rod, he shall not die. Thou shalt beat him with
> the rod, and shalt deliver his soul from hell.
>
> Proverbs 23:13, 14
>
> The rod and reproof give wisdom: but a child left to him-
> self bringeth his mother to shame . . . Correct thy son, and
> he shall give thee rest, yea, he shall give delight unto thy
> soul.   Proverbs 29:15-17
>
> Discipline your son in his early years while there is hope.
> If you don't you will ruin his life.
>
> Proverbs 19:18 (*The Living Bible*)

Notice the purpose of discipline; it should:

1. give wisdom (Proverbs 29:15 and Ephesians 6:4).
2. avoid the shaming of the parents (Proverbs 29:15).
3. keep the child from hell (Proverbs 23:13, 14).
4. avoid ruining the child's life (Proverbs 19:18).

In other words, discipline is for our children's good. It is
essential if our children are to live happy lives on earth
and also be prepared for heaven.

[3] Proverbs 22:6, "Train up a child in the way he should go: and when
he is old, he will not depart from it."

But the importance of discipline does not end here. *God has established parental authority to teach children respect for other authority.* The Bible teaches that all authority is given by God. This includes the authority of pastors, teachers, slave owners, parents, and civil leaders. Romans 13:1 says, "Let every soul be subject unto the higher powers. For there is no power but of God: the powers that be are ordained of God." 1 Timothy 6:1, 2 tells slaves to be obedient to their masters so that the Gospel will not be blasphemed. [4] Ephesians 6:1 tells of a child's responsibility to his parents. [5] Ephesians 5:24 tells wives to be in submission to their husbands. [6]

In every instance we are told to be in submission to authority. Notice that the correctness of the behavior of the authority is not in question. God does not say, "Obey your parents as long as they are correct," or "Obey the government as long as you agree!" Instead, He tells even slaves to be obedient to their masters! First Peter 2:13-15 says, "Submit yourselves to every ordinance of man for the Lord's sake: whether it be to the king, as supreme; or unto governors, as unto them that are sent by him for the punishment of evildoers, and for the praise of them that do well. For so is the will of God, that with well-doing ye may put to silence the ignorance of foolish men."

The reason for this line of authority is twofold. *First, society must have structure to exist.* Without respect for authority, society is thrown into chaos. If children do not

[4] "Let as many servants as are under the yoke count their own masters worthy of all honour, that the name of God and his doctrine be not blasphemed. And they that have believing masters, let them not despise them because they are brethren, but rather do them service, because they are faithful and beloved, partakers of the benefit. These things teach and exhort."

[5] "Children, obey your parents in the Lord: for this is right."

[6] "Therefore, as the church is subject unto Christ, so let the wives be to their own husbands in every thing."

learn to obey authority, our society will collapse. Individuals will fail to develop respect for authority in general and for God in particular. As a matter of fact, this is precisely the situation in the world today. We have reared a generation of self-centered youth who have not learned to accept authority. Now we are reaping the fruit of our permissiveness.

God has a divine plan for the ages. It spans from creation to eternity and includes both nations and individuals. *Another reason for the line of earthly authority is to achieve His purpose in human history.* To accomplish this, God sets up rulers and puts them down again. All of human history is in His hand. By obeying legal authority we aid in carrying out God's plan. The intriguing history of the nation of Israel is just one example of His divine design for man.

These concepts illustrate the tremendous importance of proper discipline. If we fail to set reasonable limits, we train children for lawless lives and irresponsible conduct.

DISCIPLINE AND PUNISHMENT

An important point for a biblical view on child rearing is to distinguish between punishment and discipline. Billy, for example, had just pulled all the mixing bowls from the kitchen cupboard. Discovering the mess, Mrs. Martin said angrily, "How many times have I told you to stay out of there? You deserve a spanking!" With that she gave Billy a few good swats and sent him to his room. Head down and teary-eyed, Billy headed for bed. *Mrs. Martin was punishing Billy for his actions.*

Contrast this with a similar scene at the Harris home. Little Raymond had just emptied the contents of mother's cupboard onto the floor. Arriving on the scene Mrs. Harris said in a calm but firm voice, "Raymond, mother has told you not to put her pans on the floor. Mother will have to spank you so you will remember not to do it again!" With that she gave Raymond a few good swats and said lovingly, "Now let's help mother pick them up." Raymond cried a little, then helped his mother pick things up. *Mrs. Harris was successfully disciplining her child.*

These situations were similar and both children were physically spanked. But there were some major differences. Mrs. Martin spanked Billy as a penalty for misdeeds. Mrs. Harris spanked Raymond, but for a different reason. She was not trying to get revenge or even the score for bad behavior. She was training him to be obedient for his own good. God deals this way with us. As His children, we are

disciplined to learn and to grow. But we are not punished
to even the score for our disobedience.

God punishes non-Christians for their sins. But all of His
punishment toward believers' sins was suffered by Christ
on the cross. Compare the following passages and you can
begin to see the differences between God's punishment of
the non-Christian and God's discipline of His children.

To God's Children (Discipline):
> My son, despise not the *chastening* of the Lord; neither be
> weary of his *correction*. For whom the Lord loveth he cor-
> recteth; even as a father the son in whom he delighteth.
> Proverbs 3:11, 12

To the Non-Christian (Punishment):
> Behold, the day of the LORD cometh, cruel both with wrath
> and fierce anger, to lay the land desolate: and he shall
> destroy the sinners thereof out of it. For the stars of heaven
> and the constellations thereof shall not give their light: the
> sun shall be darkened in his going forth, and the moon shall
> not cause her light to shine. And I will punish the world for
> their evil, and the wicked for their iniquity; and I will cause
> the arrogancy of the proud to cease, and will lay low the
> haughtiness of the terrible. Isaiah 13:9-11

To God's Children (Discipline):
> As many as I love, I rebuke and chasten: be zealous there-
> fore, and repent. Revelation 3:19

To the Non-Christian (Punishment):
> And these shall go away into everlasting punishment: but
> the righteous into life eternal. Matthew 25:46

To God's Children (Discipline):
> So also Christ died only once as an offering for the sins of
> many people; and *He will come again, but not to deal again
> with our sins.* This time He will come bringing salvation to
> all those who are eagerly and patiently waiting for Him.
> Hebrews 9:28 (*The Living Bible*)

This passage is contrasting the Old Testament sacrificial
system with the new covenant system of Grace. Under

the old system the high priest entered the inner room of the tabernacle once a year to cover the sins of the people of Israel. Under the new system Christ paid the penalties of sin once and for all.

To the Non-Christian (Punishment):

> And to you who are troubled rest with us, when the Lord Jesus shall be revealed from heaven with his mighty angels, *in flaming fire taking vengeance on them that know not God,* and that obey not the gospel of our Lord Jesus Christ: who shall be punished with everlasting destruction from the presence of the Lord, and from the glory of his power.
>
> 2 Thessalonians 1:7-9

To God's Children (Discipline):

> My son, regard not lightly the chastening of the Lord, Nor faint when thou art reproved of him; For whom the Lord loveth he chasteneth, And scourgeth every son whom he receiveth.
>
> Bear what you have to bear as "chastening" — as God's dealing with you as sons. No true son ever grows up uncorrected by his father. For if you had no experience of the correction which all sons have to bear you might well doubt the legitimacy of your sonship. After all, when we were children we had fathers who corrected us, and we respected them for it. Can we not much more readily submit to the discipline of the Father of men's souls, and learn how to live?
>
> For our fathers used to correct us according to their own ideas during the brief days of childhood. But God corrects us all our days *for our own benefit* to teach us his holiness.
>
> Hebrews 12:5-10 (Phillips)

To the Non-Christian (Punishment):

> The Lord knoweth how to deliver the godly out of temptations and to reserve the unjust unto the day of judgment to be punished.　　　2 Peter 2:9

In God's dealings with man there is a clear distinction between punishment as a means of administering just retribution for misdeeds, and discipline which is designed to promote the growth of the disciplined one. All of God's righteous demands were met by Christ's atoning death on the cross. Justice for man's misdeeds was satisfied once and for all. When we accept Christ as personal Savior we receive no more punishment. That is reserved for those who do not appropriate Christ's payment for sins.

This doesn't imply that God does not discipline, chasten, or correct His children. Surely He does. The difference is that discipline is not a means of justice. Justice has already been accomplished. Discipline is God's way of maturing His children. *Discipline* is instruction or training designed to correct misbehavior and develop the disciplined one. It doesn't involve justice, punishment, or getting even. *Punishment* is a penalty inflicted on an offender as retribution. Punishment has justice as its goal, not reformation or personal growth.

Unfortunately, most English Bible translations use "discipline" and "punishment" interchangeably. Consequently, some passages read as though God is punishing the Christian. This is not so. A careful reading of the context and usage of the words "punish" and "discipline," along with an awareness of the different principles involved, will help avoid confusion on this point. The differences between punishment and discipline are summarized in the following table:

TABLE 1

PUNISHMENT AND DISCIPLINE

	Punishment	Discipline
Purpose	To inflict penalty for an offense	To train for correction and maturity
Focus	Past misdeeds	Future correct deeds
Attitude	Hostility and frustration on the part of the parent	Love and concern on the part of the parent
Resulting Emotion in the Child	Fear and guilt	Security

Now let's make this practical. God never says to you, "I am angry! You sinned against Me and I am going to get even by spanking you!" Instead, He says, "You have sinned. I took out all of My anger toward your sin at the cross. I love you and you are My child. Since you are My child I am going to discipline you to help you grow and mature."

Barbara was a Christian woman who had some very negative childhood experiences. Her father drank heavily and had many problems. Barbara's poor relationship with her earthly father carried over into her relationship with God. She feared Him greatly. She told me how she tried to have devotions, but her prayers didn't seem to go beyond the roof. Nothing seemed to work. Sensing her unhealthy fear of God, I said, "Why don't you forget devotions for awhile?" She immediately exclaimed, "If I didn't have daily devotions I would be afraid God would strike me dead!" Then she broke into tears. Such fear! Barbara's image of God was like her harsh, punitive father. She thought God was a "get even" God.

After working through the feelings toward her father, Barbara began to understand God's loving discipline of His children. She came to realize that all of her sins had been paid for two thousand years ago. Her reason for reading the Bible and praying should not be fear of a vengeful God. She should want to fellowship because of His great love. One morning Barbara entered my office with a radiant smile. She said happily, "I had meaningful devotions for the first time in my life this morning!" "Why?" I asked. "I just wanted to get to know my heavenly Father!" she replied.

Barbara was learning about her heavenly Father. She was finding out He does not punish His children. He loves them. And when that love requires discipline, He does it lovingly.

But what does this mean in regard to our children? Simply this. *We should never punish our children to get even.* How many times have we spanked our children because we wanted them to "pay for their sins"? Let's say you have the house ready for company and your child spills milk on the rug. You say, "Janie! Look what you've done! I just finished cleaning! Now go to your room and don't come out till I tell you!"

Let's look at your reaction. You were angry because Janie disobeyed. She caused you more work. Being angry, you tried to get even by sending her to bed. Through this, Janie was probably developing a fear of you. She knew you were punishing her in anger rather than instructing her in love.

Punishment and fear of punishment may temporarily bring about desired behavior. But when they do, the final result is bad. Do you get much reward when your son says, "I'll do what you want, because you will spank me hard if I don't!"? Of course not! He obeys only out of fear. But how do you feel when your child says, "Sure, daddy! I'd like to do that, because I love you!" Think how it must be with God! He lovingly longs for the obedience of His children. He warns them of the consequence of misbehavior. And He disciplines. But He does not threaten us into good behavior by the use of His power. Listen to God's viewpoint on motivation by fear and punishment.

> God is love, and whoever lives in love lives in God and God lives in him. This is the purpose of love being made perfect in us: it is that we may be full of courage on Judgment Day, because our life in this world is the same as Christ's. *There is no fear in love; perfect love drives out all fear.* So then, love has not been made perfect in the one who fears, because *fear has to do with punishment.*
>
> 1 John 4:16-18 (*Good News for Modern Man*)

This passage is saying that God never motivates us by *fear or punishment*. This may be a startling concept since we are so used to feeling that He does! Even our churches sometimes depict God as a frightening father figure who is closely scrutinizing our every action. In Sunday school we are taught the little song:

> "*Be careful* little eyes what you see;
> *Be careful* little eyes what you see;
> For the Father up above
> Is looking down in love.
> So, *be careful* little eyes what you see.
>
> *Be careful* little ears what you hear;
> *Be careful* little ears what you hear;
> For the Father up above
> Is looking down in love.
> So, *be careful* little ears what you hear.
>
> *Be careful* little tongue what you say;
> *Be careful* little tongue what you say;
> For the Father up above
> Is looking down in love.
> So, *be careful* little tongue what you say.
>
> *Be careful* little hands what you do;
> *Be careful* little hands what you do;
> For the Father up above
> Is looking down in love.
> So, *be careful* little hands what you do.
>
> *Be careful* little feet where you go;
> *Be careful* little feet where you go;
> For the Father up above
> Is looking down in love.
> So, *be careful* little feet where you go."

Although this song mentions the love of God and is pointing out God's concern with sin it also has a bad effect. To an overly sensitive child it says, "You'd better watch out for God. He knows everything you do and can't wait to get even. He really seems to enjoy punishing little children." Children should not be taught to be obedient because God is watching their every move. They should be taught to obey because God loves them and they want to respond to that love. Fear-motivation has caused many Christians to lose out on a vital relationship with a loving heavenly Father.

Have you ever sinned and had that vague, fearful thought, "Sometime, somehow, God is going to get even"? This is natural, since most of us were brought up on a "balanced scale" system. Each time we misbehaved the scale tipped to the "bad behavior" side. To even the scale, we were punished. Then the scale read, "Accounts even — punishment has been paid." As Christians we carry this "balanced scale" idea over to God. We feel we deserve punishment to balance the scale. We have a vague expectancy of punishment or a feeling of self-condemnation. We actually want to be punished to relieve our false sense of guilt. We forget that for all those who trust in Christ, God balanced the scale once and for all two thousand years ago.

Sometimes it takes months or even years to overcome the feeling that God is a "get even" God. We find it hard to realize He deeply desires holy living but that His method is discipline, not punishment, and that His motivation is love, not fear. Even though we "know" intellectually that God loves us, we may have trouble "feeling" His acceptance. We tell ourselves, "God has forgiven." But our emotions cry out, "Don't believe it! You are bad. You deserve to be punished." It takes a great deal of biblical understanding and emotional growth to feel at a deep level that God accepts us completely. It takes time to feel that He never wants to even the score, that He is never angry and that He never motivates by fear.

Realizing the great difficulties we have had in learning
this truth, let's give our children a biblical pattern. Then
they can more easily see the beautiful plan of God's divine
discipline.

TEACHING RESPECT WITHOUT INSTILLING FEAR

To understand God's plan for discipline, we must have a
clear conception of fear and respect. The Bible has two
meanings for the word "fear." *In some cases fear means a
form of anxiety, a harmful emotion. At other times it is
used in a positive way to mean respect.* In these following
passages "fear" is used to mean a reverential trust in God.

> The *fear of the* LORD is the beginning of wisdom: and the
> knowledge of the holy is understanding.   Proverbs 9:10
> The *fear of the* LORD tendeth to life: and he that hath it
> shall abide satisfied; he shall not be visited with evil.
> Proverbs 19:23

In other passages, such as 1 John 4:18 and those applying to the non-Christian's fear of God, there is a conno-
tation of anxiety and fearfulness. [7] *The Christian is to have
a reverential trust in God, but he should never be afraid of
the Lord!*

Likewise, *a child should trust and respect his parents.
But he should never fear them!* Some insecure parents exert
their power by severely punishing a child. They think they
are teaching obedience and respect, but they are actually
instilling a negative, neurotic fear. When we punish children

[7] 1 John 4:18, "There is no fear in love; but perfect love casteth out
fear: because fear hath torment. He that feareth is not made perfect in
love.
Hebrews 10:31, "It is a fearful thing to fall into the hands of the living
God."
Romans 8:15, "For ye have not received the spirit of bondage again to
fear; but ye have received the Spirit of adoption, whereby we cry, Abba,
Father."
2 Timothy 1:7, "For God hath not given us the spirit of fear; but of
power, and of love, and of a sound mind."

in anger, we promote this negative fear and erect barriers between ourselves and our children. Even though they obey, they find it difficult to communicate freely because of fear. Children need to respect their parents. But respect must be earned through respectful living. It cannot be "won" through power! A child may learn that he can't "sass" his parents without getting clobbered. So he stops sassing or retreats a few feet before making his remarks. But what has been accomplished? The child fears his parents' power but inwardly has even less respect. How can he respect an adult who is angered by a childish attack on his self-esteem? He really can't. The way to win respect is to hear your child out. If he is upset, let him tell you. If you allow expression of his true feelings, you are showing respect. When you respect your child, he returns the favor.

This doesn't mean we allow unbridled verbal or physical expression. There are times when each of us, including children, must restrain our feelings. But in an intimate parent-child relation, there should be complete freedom to express negative emotions verbally. If a child's language is crude, you may suggest a better way of self-expression. A mother recently told me her son was continually telling his sister, "I hate you!" This upset the sister and her mother. To solve the problem, the mother suggested Teddy say, "Right now I am very upset with you!" This allowed expression of his strong feelings but avoided the hurt of "hate." At no time should we deprive children of their feelings. This is disrespectful and only breeds stronger hostility.

There is also a difference between fearfulness and respect for negative consequences. We call both of these fear, although one is positive and the other negative. For example, let's take crossing the street safely. You obviously don't want your child to learn this lesson through the natural consequence of being hit by a car. You have two ways of teaching him respect for traffic. One approach is to shout, "Look out! Here comes a car!" as you cross the street. By using this approach you will teach your child to be careful when he crosses the street. But *you are also making him fearful and anxious.* This is similar to a frightened mother who hides her children in a corner during a thunderstorm!

There is a better way to teach your child to be careful. This is to tell him *calmly,* "We look both ways before we cross the street." By looking both ways and calmly telling him to do so, too, you teach *your child to be careful without learning to be afraid!* This is God's method with us. He tells us there are bad results from sin. But He does not anxiously shout in our ear each time we are about to do wrong. Neither does He scare us with threats of punishment. The order of God's discipline runs like this:

1. He saves us and removes all punishment for our sins on the basis of Christ's atoning death on the cross.
2. He sets guidelines for behavior which are not His personal whims but which are for our good and in accordance with His holy nature.
3. He tells of the negative consequences of sin, but does not threaten us with punishment or rejection.
4. When we sin He often uses natural consequences to allow us to learn through our mistakes.
5. When He needs to intervene in discipline, He does it calmly, and in love. He disciplines to correct and instruct us, not to vent His anger or gain revenge.

Isn't God a great Parent! He really trains us for *our* own good! *He never takes out His frustrations on us!* And He patiently guides us to maturity. Think of what we can learn from this. Our homes can be revolutionized when we begin to apply methods of discipline in the same spirit in which He disciplines us!

WHAT ABOUT **MY** FEELINGS?

This pattern of discipline sounds great, but we aren't God. Sometimes we do get angry. Sometimes we do want revenge. Sometimes we do take out our frustrations, even if it isn't for our children's good. As a matter of fact, some "authorities" on child rearing recommend that parents ventilate their anger. One modern author writes:

> Some of you may have heard the old saying, "Never strike a child in anger." I think that is psychologically very poor advice, and I suggest the opposite: "Never strike a child except in anger" . . . What I advocate is the "pow-wow" type of spanking: your "pow" followed by his "wow"! Spank your child only when you are furious at him and feel like letting him have it right then. Too many mothers nowadays seem to be afraid to spank their children. They talk and nag a great deal as a substitute; they try to negotiate with a child . . . . What you should do is tell your child once or perhaps twice what you want him to do or to stop doing. Then, if he refuses to obey your reasonable request, and you have become frustrated and angry, let him have it right then and there. [8]

Dr. Haim Ginott, author of the best selling, *Between Parent and Child,* suggests that parents express their angry feelings by statements such as, "It makes me mad to see that!" "It makes me angry," or "It makes me furious!" [9]

The point these men are making is not that parents should stir up anger to ventilate on children. They are trying to point out that parents are people, too. All of us have times of frustration and anger. And we should not condemn ourselves for negative emotions. They are a part of life and we should accept them. But we should not deny

[8] *How to Parent,* Fitzhugh Dodson, Los Angeles: Nash Publishing Co., 1970, p. 207.

[9] *Between Parent and Child,* Haim Ginott, New York: Macmillan, 1965, p. 105.

the bad effects of anger just to soothe our parental con-
sciences. Here are a few biblical comments on hostility.

> Cease from anger, and forsake wrath: fret not thyself in
> any wise to do evil.   Psalm 37:8

> Remember this, my dear brothers! Everyone must be quick
> to listen, but slow to speak, and slow to become angry. *For
> man's anger does not help to achieve God's righteous pur-
> poses.* Rid yourselves, then, of every filthy habit and all
> wicked conduct. Submit to God and accept the word that
> he plants in your hearts, which is able to save you.
>
>   James 1:19-21 (*Good News for Modern Man*)

The Bible makes it clear that anger is sin and should be
resolved. (This is more fully dealt with in chapter eleven.)
This certainly applies to the intimate relationship of a
parent and a child. God has not only given a pattern of
discipline; He has given specific commandments that we
should put away our anger. But we must close our discussion of anger for the time being. Part 4, "Parents Are
People, Too," goes into detail on how we can handle
our own feelings. For now, we want to make one point.
*When we spank a child in anger, we are working on our
problem, not his.* We are punishing and looking for revenge, rather than disciplining out of love. We shouldn't
kid ourselves into thinking, "I'm doing it for his good"!

SUMMARY

Now that we have studied a number of biblical and
psychological principles, let's summarize the contents of
this chapter.

1. God instituted family life to meet our needs, teach us
   about Himself, and train children for maturity and
   righteousness.

2. God has given authority to parents, teachers, pastors, and civic leaders.

3. The purposes of this authority are to maintain society, teach respect for God's authority, and accomplish God's purpose for humanity.

4. Although Satan misguides many authorities, God works even this for good.

5. Children must be disciplined to learn wisdom, goodness, and respect.

6. God's methods of dealing with us can serve as models for our relationships with children.

7. The purpose of punishment is justice and revenge. God does not punish His children, and we should not punish ours.

8. The purpose of discipline is to train for maturity and for the child's best interests.

9. Punishment involves feelings of anger, whereas discipline is a sign of love.

10. Fear is an unhealthy motivation. God does not motivate His sons this way, and neither should we.

11. Parents should set limits for children and discipline for disobedience.

PART 2

Shaping Your Child's Behavior

The most pressing problem for modern parents is how to control their children. Temper tantrums, crying spells, and disobedience are common fare in many homes. These problems are so common they seem almost "normal." But they can be overcome. This section shows how to help your child develop more acceptable behavior patterns. It discusses seven methods of discipline and gives practical suggestions on the application of each method.

Chapter 4

PROBLEMS DON'T "JUST HAPPEN"

During a parents' seminar, the father of a ten-year-old thumb-sucker said, "I don't know how she got that habit. Why is it children act that way?" He was baffled by his child's behavior. He couldn't understand why she would "act that way." Many of us have similar frustrations. We have a hard time understanding our children's behavior. And this is normal. Human actions have many causes and seem complex. But they can be understood. This chapter gives a few basic principles which help us understand "why children act that way."

REINFORCEMENT AND EXTINCTION

Each of your child's actions has a purpose. Soon after birth he learns that some behaviors fulfill his goals. He also finds that others do not. Actions that fail to serve his purposes are dropped. Those that are successful remain. Psychologists call this type of learning, reward or reinforcement. *When your child's behavior is rewarded, the same behavior is likely to recur.* When behavior is not rewarded, it is less likely to happen again. Your child learns behaviors that meet his needs and those that don't.

Take crying, for example. You have just told your five-year-old he cannot have a popsicle before dinner. He breaks loudly into tears. You've had a hard day and can't stand this added clamor. To keep a little peace, you give in and say reluctantly, "O.K. just this once!" What have you taught your son? Unknowingly, you have taught him that crying is a good way to get his way with mom and dad. Crying was rewarded with a popsicle. Next time he wants a popsicle your son will probably cry again!

But what if you hadn't given in to the crying? Your child's behavior would be less likely to recur. Psychologists call this weakening of behavior, extinction. *When a negative behavior repeatedly fails to be rewarded, it is gradually extinguished.*

There are two major types of reinforcers. Human actions, such as hugging, talking, praising, and listening, are known as *social reinforcers. Nonsocial reinforcers* are objects or non-human activities that are rewarding. These include things like candy, money, and toys.

One Saturday morning your twelve-year-old "picks up" her room and arranges things neatly. After this she straightens the family room and helps in the kitchen. You should praise her for this good behavior. You might say, "Thank you for straightening the family room, Martha. I surely appreciate your help." Along with the praise, you could give her a big hug. The praise and the hug would be *social reinforcers.* You might also say, "Since you helped me so much, let's go downtown and get that new pair of shoes you've been talking about." The new shoes would be a *nonsocial reinforcer.* By using both social and nonsocial rewards, you are making it more likely that Martha will help you clean the house again. If Martha cleans the house and is not rewarded, she may decide it isn't worth it. She doesn't profit from her actions. There is, of course, the natural reward of living in a clean home. But for most children this is not enough!

This isn't to say we should buy our children something

every time they behave correctly. That is obviously impossible. The point is, there are practical ways of rewarding children. One of these is through a new toy, money, or an article of clothing. Chapter eight on "Choosing the 'Right' Method of Discipline," goes into more detail on the pros and cons of using money as rewards.

Sometimes we don't realize the things that are rewarding to our children. Take spanking, for example. *We* look at spankings as a form of punishment. We wonder why some children egg us into spanking them. It doesn't make sense from our perspective. But from the viewpoint of rewards, the mystery is solved. Even though a spanking is unpleasant, some children are willing to endure pain to receive the reward of parental attention. We think spankings weaken negative behavior. Actually, our increased attention may encourage future misconduct.

That raises the question of the wisdom of spankings. This will be dealt with more thoroughly in chapter six. For the present, there are two possible solutions to a child's seeking attention through spanking. One approach is to avoid rewarding the child. You can do this by simply ignoring the behavior and failing to give the desired spanking. The other alternative is to make the spanking so hard the child is unwilling to endure the pain to receive desired attention. There are appropriate times for each of these methods.

THE IMPORTANCE OF IMMEDIATE REWARDS

In teaching new behavior, parents should reward children soon after each desired act. We shouldn't wait several days to praise our daughter and buy her new shoes for cleaning the house. Immediate rewards are most effective. As a wife, you are encouraged when your husband compliments you on a new hair style. His social reinforcement makes you want to please him again. But if he waited until your hair was frazzled and said, "Honey, your hair sure looked nice last week," you wouldn't be overjoyed! When a man mows the yard, he wants immediate reward for his labor. By bringing a coke and saying, "The yard looks terrific," his wife is giving both social and nonsocial reinforcement immediately after the desired behavior. He will be more likely to mow the yard again because of the rewards!

NEGATIVE REINFORCERS

Actions that stop annoying experiences also serve as reinforcers. When a radio is blaring (annoying experience) you can reach over and turn it off. Your act of turning off the radio is rewarded by the removal of an annoying situation. Because your behavior terminated a negative experience, this is called a negative reinforcement. A nagging mother brings on negative reinforcement. The nagging (annoying experience) may cause children to stop objectionable behavior. They are sick and tired of mother's complaining; so they finally stop. Their behavior is much like turning off a radio. It removes a negative experience. Though the negative behavior sometimes ceases, nagging is not a good way to change behavior. It usually builds hostile feelings and complicates your problems in the long run.

OCCASIONAL REINFORCEMENT

Under certain conditions children should be rewarded every time they repeat a desired activity. At other times they learn better by periodic reinforcement. When they are learning *new* behavior, children should be rewarded every time they perform a desired task. Let's say you are teaching your three-year-old to dress himself. Each time he puts on his clothes he needs some reinforcement. You might say, "That's good, Marty! You're sure a big boy!"

After behavior has been well established it is *not* necessary to reward it every time. Research studies show that once behavior becomes a habit it is actually better to reinforce it only on occasion. This means that in teaching your child to dress, you would begin by rewarding him every time he put on his clothes. After he routinely dressed himself, you should then praise him only on occasion.

LEARNING STEP BY STEP

The size of the task to be rewarded influences the amount of learning. In dressing, for example, you may start by rewarding your child for merely bringing you his clothes. After he has done that, you might reward him for putting on his pants. After mastering these tasks, you could withhold reinforcement until he learned to tie his shoes. Finally, you would reward him for dressing himself completely.

We fail to complete some jobs because they seem so big. They take too long and rewards seem far away. By breaking big jobs into little parts, we can reward for each small step. By our use of this procedure, children will gradually be ready for the total task.

IMITATION

"Do as I say, not as I do." This parental proverb is an unspoken command of many parents. Unfortunately, it doesn't work! Children learn more from our behavior than from any other source. All of the preaching and teaching in the world is overshadowed by our actions.

Imitating parents is a basic form of learning. Your child develops a masculine or feminine identity largely through imitation. You can't really teach a girl to become a woman. She picks it up from mother. Neither can you teach a boy to be a man. But as he identifies with father, he models his behavior after this respected adult. He gradually takes on dad's masculine behavior. Masculine and feminine roles are also reinforced by good relations with the parent of the opposite sex.

Yelling, pouting, and other negative reactions are also learned from parents. To guide children into mature Christian character, we must start with ourselves. As we set a good example, children go that way.

HOW CHILDREN TRAIN THEIR PARENTS

"Mark, it's time for dinner," Mr. Perry called in a normal voice. When Mark failed to respond and reward his father by coming, Mr. Perry called a little louder, "Mark, it's time for dinner!" When there was still no response Mr. Perry shouted, "Mark! Get in here this minute!!!" Finally Mark dragged in. Let's evaluate this scene. By not seeing to it that Mark came on his first call, Mr. Perry taught Mark he could play a little longer. He rewarded Mark's dawdling behavior with extra play time. He taught Mark he was not really expected to come until the third shout. This is bad enough. *But look at what Mark was teaching his father.* Mark failed to reward his dad by coming when he called in a normal voice. This weakened Mr. Perry's calm behavior. By finally coming when he shouted, Mark reinforced his father's anger! The next time he calls Mark to dinner, Mr. Perry will be more likely to yell. That behavior was rewarded, but his pleasant request was not. Reinforcement is not a one-sided venture. *Children also teach parents good and bad behavior.*

Nagging is another example of the way children teach parents. On Friday evening mother says, "Remember, Dave, you're to take out the trash tomorrow." Saturday morning she reminds him again, "Don't forget the trash." Later in the day she asks anxiously, "Have you taken care of the trash yet?" Finally Dave says a disgusted "O.K.!" and empties the trash. Mother thinks Dave did it because she reminded him three or four times. Her nagging is reinforced. She thinks, "I told him four times and he took out the trash. My nagging works. Next time I will nag some more." Dave is teaching his mother she must nag to get him to work. This process is upsetting to both Dave and his mother. How much better if Dave could be taught to carry out the trash on his own. Mother should not allow Dave to reinforce her bad behavior. Dave needs to learn his own responsibilities. Chapter five, in the section on "Logical Consequences," gives some specific suggestions for handling this type of problem.

REVIEW OF LEARNING PRINCIPLES

Let's summarize the principles of learning we have discussed so far:

1. Actions that are reinforced are more likely to be repeated in the future.
2. Behaviors that are not rewarded tend to weaken and become extinguished.

3. A reinforcement is anything that satisfies a goal or leads to pleasure.
4. A social reinforcer is any type of human relationship with a positive value to a child.
5. A nonsocial reinforcer is any nonhuman object or experience which the child enjoys.
6. To be most effective, reinforcements should come soon after the desired behavior.
7. Actions that stop painful experiences also serve as reinforcers. These are called negative reinforcers.
8. When your child is learning a new behavior, it is important to reward him every time he performs the task.
9. After desirable behavior is learned, it should be reinforced only on occasion.
10. When teaching new behaviors, it helps to break a large task into several smaller steps and give reinforcement after each one.
11. Parents often unconsciously reinforce undesirable actions, such as crying, even though they don't approve of such behavior.
12. Children reinforce undesirable behavior in parents and promote continued family problems.

To illustrate the use of these principles, let's look at two common family problems.

TEACHING TABLE MANNERS BY REINFORCEMENT AND EXTINCTION

In the following example each statement has been given a number. The number agrees with one of the twelve principles of learning summarized above. Reviewing the principles in the illustrations will help clarify the use of rewards and extinction.

Mr. and Mrs. Andrews were trying to teach their son some table manners. One evening Jimmy said, "Dad, gimme some more bread!" Mr. Andrews handed Jimmy the bread and

reminded him, "You should say, 'please pass the bread.'"
Unknowingly, he was reinforcing Jimmy's bad manners (1
& 11). Mr. Andrews shouldn't have passed the bread when
Jimmy said, "gimme." If he had ignored the request or
calmly stated, "We do not pass things unless you ask polite-
ly," Mr. Andrews would not have rewarded Jimmy's impo-
liteness. The chances of his saying "gimme" at another meal
would have lessened (2). If Jimmy later said, "Mom, please
pass the milk," Mrs. Andrews should pass the milk and compliment him for being polite. In this way she would reinforce the desired behavior (1) with both a nonsocial reinforcer (milk, 4) and a social reinforcer (compliment, 5). By
passing food soon after each polite request, the Andrews
would be encouraging polite behavior by immediately reinforcing Jimmy (6) and by rewarding him each time he
showed polite behavior (8). After Jimmy acquired the habit
of saying "please" it would not be necessary to reward him
with praise each time he was polite. The nonsocial reward
of receiving the food and an occasional social reward would
maintain the good habit (9).

SOLVING TEMPER TANTRUMS BY EXTINCTION

When Mrs. Morris said he couldn't go outside to play,
Jamie promptly threw a king sized tantrum. He screamed
at the top of his lungs, threw himself on the floor, and
seemed to become hysterical. Jamie wanted his way; so he
started a power struggle to get it. "Stop that this minute!"
his mother shouted. "I won't!" screamed Jamie. And the
battle was on! (Jamie had already won, of course, since
mother had lost her cool!) Having all she could take, Mrs.
Morris gave Jamie a swift right to the bottom. Jamie yelled
louder. Finally Mrs. Morris sent Jamie to his room. There he
screamed another twenty minutes. When Mr. Morris arrived
home his wife said in defeat, "I don't know what's wrong
with that child! He threw another tantrum today!"

Let's apply what we've learned so far to this behavior problem. Jamie wanted to control his mother so he could go out and play. When Mrs. Morris refused, Jamie threw a tantrum. He hoped mother would give in and let him play. Not to be defeated (she thought), Mrs. Morris refused, and spanked Jamie for his tantrum. Now Jamie was not only upset about not getting to play. He was mad at his mother for fighting back at his power play. This called for revenge — so Jamie yelled a little louder. Finally he was sent to his room. Let's summarize this battle:

1. Jamie wanted to go outside.
2. Mrs. Morris denied his wish.
3. Jamie threw a tantrum to gain power and get his way.
4. Mrs. Morris accepted Jamie's challenge to her power. She spanked him to prove she was in control.
5. Seeing his mother use her strength to fight made Jamie really angry. He retaliated by screaming louder.
6. Not to be defeated, Mrs. Morris sent Jamie to his room.
7. Not to be defeated, Jamie kept on screaming.

Did Mrs. Morris unknowingly reward any of Jamie's behavior? The first impression is no. Since Jamie didn't get to go outside he wasn't rewarded. But look again. Going out was only Jamie's initial goal. He had two more. He wanted to demonstrate his power and also get revenge. Once he provoked his mother to frustration, Jamie had shown his power. He had enticed this big, mature adult into fighting like a child! This rewarded Jamie's search for power. When he kept on screaming, Jamie gave his mother fits. She was a nervous wreck. This was sweet revenge for not letting him go outside. *Jamie was rewarded both for his desire for power and his search for revenge.* The next time a similar situation arises he will more likely have another tantrum. Mrs. Morris is unwittingly teaching Jamie to throw more tantrums.

But what could Mrs. Morris do? She could apply the principle of extinction. When a behavior is not rewarded it is weakened. It is less likely to happen again. If Jamie had not been rewarded in his search for power and revenge, his tantrums would soon have ceased. To eliminate tantrums we must do two things. *We must avoid being brought into the power struggle and we must ignore the tantrum.* Ignore that screaming? Definitely! The purpose of the tantrum is to get us into a power struggle. If we don't respond to the invitation, our children will have to battle by themselves. To be effective, a tantrum must have an audience. If your nerves can stand it, continue your work and ignore the tantrum. If it upsets you too much, go to another room. When all else fails, go to the bathroom and read a magazine! Whatever you do, don't try to force him to stop! If you do, he has drawn you into the power struggle and you have lost already!

After one mother learned to ignore her son's temper tantrums, he stopped in the middle of his act and said with surprise, "What's the matter, mom? Aren't you going to spank me?" He couldn't believe she refused to fall for his play for power!

SUMMARY

Now we can partially answer the question, *"Why is it that well-meaning parents raise children who are uncooperative and show many types of negative behavior?"* The answer is this. *We often unconsciously reward children for negative, attention-getting behavior.* Our methods of discipline and communication sometimes teach a child that he can con us into meeting his wishes by showing bad behavior. As long as these actions meet his needs, there is no reason to find more desirable ways to reach his goals. To eliminate undesirable actions, we must see that children get absolutely no reward for bad behavior. Only then are they free to learn constructive ways of meeting their needs.

Chapter 5

HOW NATURE DISCIPLINES YOUR CHILD

When our daughter was one year old she developed a habit of nibbling on soap. We told her, "No, no," spanked her, and took the soap away. But a day or so later she was up to her old tricks. One Sunday morning before church we decided to utilize natural consequences. When Debbie started nibbling, we went about our business. Soon Kathy said, "Honey, shouldn't we stop her now?" "No," I replied. "Let's wait and see what happens." We gritted our teeth and Debbie kept on chewing. Soon bubbles were coming out her mouth. After a while she began to cry. Finally, I lifted her into the bathtub and put her under the faucet. Then we used a wash cloth to help get out the soap. Debbie kept on crying, as we couldn't remove it all. Soon her lips began to swell. Now we were really feeling guilty. It seemed awful to mistreat this poor, "innocent" child. Of course, we hadn't mistreated her at all. And she really wasn't "innocent." When Debbie's lip kept swelling, Kathy phoned our physician. He reassured her that nothing serious would happen and told us to apply some vaseline. But after church Debbie was still in a bad way! Her stomach must have been upset, since she didn't eat her lunch. She seemed listless and couldn't go to sleep. It was evening before she finally started to recover.

Let me tell you, that was a rough day! We felt miserable. We looked at each other and felt like crying. How could we allow a little doll like Debbie to suffer such pain! But soon our efforts were rewarded. About one week after the soap incident Debbie was taking a bath. She picked up the soap, put it to her mouth, smelled it, looked at mother, and laid it down. Since that time she hasn't eaten soap again! Our scoldings and spankings had done no good, but when we let nature do its job, our problem was solved!

NATURAL CONSEQUENCES

Most family conflicts involve a struggle for power between
parent and child. Since the parent is stronger, he may be
able to force his desires onto the child. But this rarely solves
the problem. The power-hungry child fights back. He may
not have his way, but at least he can make his parents miserable. This starts a vicious cycle. The child misbehaves. The
parent tries to force him to conform. And the child fights
back. Once this pattern is established, little peace remains.
Every attempt at discipline degenerates into a struggle for
power. This doesn't need to happen. There are ways of ex-
tricating ourselves from battle so that we can calmly correct
our children's misbehavior. One of these methods is natural
consequences. [1] In natural consequences we simply allow
nature to run its course.

By allowing nature to do its job, we completely avoid a
power struggle. Neither parent nor child becomes angry, because there is no conflict. Not only that, the child sees clearly the reasons why he should change behaviors. He doesn't
have to stop "because daddy says so." He stops because it's
good for him. God uses the same method in dealing with us.
Consider the following verses:

> Be not deceived; God is not mocked: *for whatsoever a man
> soweth, that shall he also reap.*   Galatians 6:7
> *He that soweth iniquity shall reap vanity*: and the rod of
> his anger shall fail.   Proverbs 22:8

When God wants to teach us something, we often feel He
intervenes, uses His power, and disciplines. Sometimes He
does. But many times He allows us to learn from our mistakes. The parable of the prodigal son is a good example of

[1] The foremost proponent of natural consequences is Dr. Rudolf Dreikurs. *A Parent's Guide to Child Discipline*, co-authored by Dr. Dreikurs
and Dr. Loren Grey, is "must reading" for all parents. See chapter fourteen for further comments on this book.

natural consequences. The father in this story represents
God the Father. The son is any wayward child of God.

> And he said, A certain man had two sons: and the younger
> of them said to *his* father, Father, give me the portion of
> goods that falleth *to me*. And he divided unto them *his*
> living. And not many days after the younger son gathered
> all together, and took his journey into a far country, and
> there wasted his substance with riotous living. And when
> he had spent all, there arose a mighty famine in that land;
> and he began to be in want. And he went and joined
> himself to a citizen of that country; and he sent him into
> his fields to feed swine. And he would fain have filled his
> belly with the husks that the swine did eat: and no man
> gave unto him. And when he came to himself, he said,
> How many hired servants of my father's have bread
> enough and to spare, and I perish with hunger! I will arise
> and go to my father, and will say unto him, Father, I have
> sinned against heaven, and before thee, and am no more
> worthy to be called thy son: make me as one of thy hired
> servants. And he arose, and came to his father. But when
> he was yet a great way off, his father saw him, and had
> compassion, and ran, and fell on his neck, and kissed him.
> And the son said unto him, Father, I have sinned against
> heaven, and in thy sight, and am no more worthy to be
> called thy son. But the father said to his servants, Bring
> forth the best robe, and put *it* on him; and put a ring on
> his hand, and shoes on *his* feet: and bring hither the
> fatted calf, and kill *it;* and let us eat, and be merry: for
> this my son was dead, and is alive again; he was lost, and
> is found. And they began to be merry.   Luke 15:11-24

This young son had a problem. He was selfish, impulsive,
and given to carnal living. He decided to "live it up" and
asked his dad for his share of the family estate. Notice the
father's reaction. He knew the problems this boy was headed
for. He loved his son and wanted to help him avoid serious
problems. But he gave him the money! Why in the world
would he do a foolish thing like that? We would probably
say, "Of course you can't have the money. You're still wet

behind the ears and can't even handle your allowance. Besides that you'll get into all sorts of sin, and I don't want that to happen. When you grow up, I'll let you have your share. Now go on out to the field and work like your older brother!"

But this father took a different approach. He used natural consequences. He apparently realized his son would not "grow up" by staying home. Because the son was stubborn, he would learn only from the school of hard knocks. So the father let him go. This wasn't easy. Surely the dad was tempted to lecture the son and force him to stay home. But he knew that wouldn't work. He gave him the money, wished him well, and went on with his business.

Armed with his new-found wealth, the son headed for a far country. The farther he could get from home, the better. He was fed up with that farm and wanted to lose his identity in a foreign land. He sought out the prostitutes, boozed it up, and soon ran through his father's cash. Having no place to turn, he slopped hogs for a little spending money. Things were so bad he was tempted to eat the pig's food. Think of it! The son of a wealthy farmer was living like a bum! *This was the consequence of his behavior.* No lecture in the world would get a point across like this. Finally the son wised up. He knew his father's servants were better off than he. So he headed home to ask forgiveness.

Seeing his son walking down the road, his father ran and kissed him. He didn't say, "I told you so," and he didn't "rub it in!" I'm sure he was tempted to lecture his wayward son and extract a promise of better things. But he restrained himself. He knew the boy had learned his lesson. Rejoicing over his son's return, the father killed the fatted calf. He used no other discipline because he had utilized natural consequences. This story pictures an ideal father. His love was constant. He didn't degrade his son. And he utilized a strong natural consequence.

Don't most of us really remember nature's lessons longest? We remember them because of our personal experience. A spanking or other parental intervention works for a while. But we usually forget the lesson and remember the spanking. With natural consequences, we rarely forget the lesson. We are not learning from someone else's knowledge. We are finding out firsthand.

THE FINICKY EATER

Ronnie was a "picky" eater. He ate very little and then only with much "help" from mother. Every meal was a rerun. Mrs. Evans put a small helping of each kind of food on Ronnie's plate. Ronnie just looked at it. Mrs. Evans said, "Eat your food, Ronnie. You want to grow up and be a big boy, don't you?" Ronnie ate a bite or two and asked for some coke. "Eat your food, and you can have some," bribed Mrs. Evans. Ronnie ate a little more and then played with his fork. "Hurry up, Ronnie, or you can't have any dessert," Mrs. Evans threatened. Finally Ronnie finished half his food and his mother let him go at that.

Let's analyze this scene. What is Ronnie trying to accomplish by his eating behavior? Which of the eight needs is he trying to meet? He isn't seeking a sense of worth or perfectionism and he definitely isn't retreating for psychological safety! We have five other options. *Ronnie may be seeking love and attention.* If he ate a hearty meal, he wouldn't be the main attraction. But by playing the undernourished child, Ronnie plays on his mother's sympathy. This gets her constant attention.

Ronnie is also in a power struggle. Mrs. Evans is trying to run his life and he knows it. She is saying, "You are a weak little child. Let mother help you eat, and you can become a big boy." Ronnie unconsciously thinks, "I'll show her! I'm a big boy now! I won't do what she says! That'll show her who's boss!"

Ronnie may also be using eating to get revenge on Mrs. Evans. No one likes to be constantly nagged at mealtime. Getting sick and tired of his mother's interference, Ronnie's anger builds. A great way to get even is to refuse to eat. Mother can beg, plead, threaten, and coerce to no avail. Ronnie sees her frustration and takes pleasure in it.

In the case of each goal Ronnie is being rewarded. He gets extra attention from his mother, involves her in a power struggle to prove his strength, and gets revenge by making Mrs. Evans feel a failure. Since Ronnie is rewarded for bad behavior, he is more likely to refuse to eat at his next meal.

This, of course, is a horrible way to get a child to eat! God created the human body so that when we are hungry we want to eat. *The only way to help a child develop proper eating habits is to let nature run its course.* When Ronnie gets hungry enough, he will eat. He will not need to be reminded. When children fail to eat, we should remove all food from the table at the end of the meal. We inform children there will be no eating until next meal. Then we leave the rest to nature!

Parents are funny creatures. We nag, bribe, and punish children when all we need to do is get out of the way. Why is it we can't allow nature to run its course? There are three main reasons. First, *we often think nagging is the thing to do.* After all, isn't it a mother's job to keep her children healthy? Our own parents probably nagged us into eating, so we follow the only method that we know.

Guilt is another cause of parental pressure at mealtime. If a child is sick or undernourished, we feel guilty and a failure. By nagging and coercing we relieve our feelings of guilt. Our children may not improve. And mealtimes are a hassle. But at least we can say, "I tried my best. There was nothing more to do." That helps us relieve our guilt. But it doesn't do much for our children.

Sympathy is another reason we find it hard it apply natural consequences to eating. Around bedtime Ronnie will become hungry. He says, "My tummy hurts, mommy!" and begins to cry. Mrs. Evans starts to feel sorry and thinks, "Maybe a glass of milk will be okay." But if she gives in, Ronnie has manipulated her into a power struggle. She has interfered with natural consequences and robbed Ronnie of a valuable lesson.

To force a child to go to bed hungry seems cruel. But remember, *we* are not forcing him to go to bed hungry. *He* forced it on himself. The price he pays for attention, power, and revenge is going to bed hungry. It won't take long for Ronnie to realize the price is too high.

"But what about his health? You can't just let him starve!"
This is a frequent reaction to this application of natural consequences. And it sounds like a valid point. But let's look a
little closer. We are not using natural consequences to deprive a child of food. We are using this discipline to teach
children to eat well, and in a peaceful manner. Can we tolerate a few missed meals to teach our children good eating
habits? What effect is the continual mealtime conflict having
on the health of his personality, not to mention the peace of
mind of the rest of the family? We must learn to tolerate our
fears and guilt for a couple of meals to avoid months or even
years of harmful emotional consequences.

But it isn't enough to have a child miss a meal for being
late. We must plan a complete approach for developing
good eating habits. As parents, we have two major duties as
far as our children's diet is concerned. *We should provide a
healthy diet and see that they don't solve their hunger needs
with "junk" between meals.* To accomplish the first, we need
only to give a basic diet. We should be sensitive to childish
tastes, since there are some things children do not like. Nothing is really gained by forcing a child to eat a vegetable he
detests. This merely starts a power struggle. We try to force
a child to eat, and he responds by refusing to cooperate. To
avoid this struggle, we should concentrate on things children enjoy even though we feel their tastes are "narrow."
By providing enjoyable foods we encourage healthy eating.

Our second responsibility is to limit between-meal snacks.
When children eat a normal meal, a snack is fine. But when
they pick at mealtime food and then stuff themselves with
candy throughout the day, nothing will be gained. We
should calmly state our eating rule. We should say, "If you
eat a good meal, you can have an occasional snack. If you
fail to eat your meal, there will be no snacks." This is a
logical consequence. But be careful. We shouldn't bribe our

children by saying, "Remember, no snacks unless you finish your meal." When we say that, we are still in a power struggle. We are trying to force a child to eat. *Remember, it is not our duty to get a child to eat.* God gave all children a built-in reminder. Our responsibility is to provide food and limit "junk." Our child's responsibility is to eat when he is ready.

The use of natural consequences is an amazingly successful way of dealing with children. Months and even years of hassles can be brought to an abrupt end when we extricate ourselves from power struggles with our children. Children are not dumb! When they see we aren't going to control their lives, they begin to assume responsibility. Behaviors that cause them hurt or pain are soon given up for more positive ways of family living.

Natural consequences can be utilized in nearly every realm of behavior where there are negative consequences. We should seldom resort to other means of discipline when natural consequences will do the job. This method teaches responsibility and self-discipline, whereas direct parental use of power only "shows a child who's boss."

LOGICAL CONSEQUENCES

The use of logical consequences is another form of discipline. The idea is similar to natural consequences. The object is to avoid a power struggle by letting children learn from the consequences of their own behavior. We replace force with consequences.

Logical consequences differ from natural consequences in one respect. In logical consequences we must be involved in structuring the consequence of misbehavior. In natural consequences we don't structure the consequence since the painful result is naturally built in.

Discipline by logical consequences also implies another

concept. The negative consequences of misbehavior should be "logically" related to the deed. To "ground" a teenager for failure to clean his room doesn't seem logical. Cleaning a room has little to do with nighttime privileges. "Grounding" would be a good "logical" consequence for a teenager who failed to keep an agreed-on curfew time. "Grounding" is logically related to failure to keep the curfew.

MEALTIME ROUNDUP

Mr. and Mrs. Benton had a rough time rounding up their four children for supper. Mrs. Benton would start calling the kids around 5:30 to get them to the table by 6:00. If the children happened to come by 5:30, they were disappointed. Their mother didn't expect them and hadn't finished preparing supper yet! After several years of this hassle, Mr. and Mrs. Benton learned the principle of logical consequences.

What would be a logical consequence for not arriving for supper on time? The answer was obvious. No supper! But this seemed cruel. What if they were only a *little* late? Should they really use such drastic measures for this common problem? Mr. and Mrs. Benton were sick and tired of playing "Dragnet" every evening to find the kids. They decided to go ahead with logical consequences. They told their children they didn't think they should have to call repeatedly every night. They felt the children could take the responsibility for making it to supper. Mother would call once five minutes before supper. Anyone who was not in place by the time dad finished praying would have to do without until the next meal.

The first night everyone was there. But the next night Mark was at a neighbor's. He came in several minutes late. Mrs. Benton felt a twinge of sorrow. Should she really carry through? She wanted to say, "O.K., just this once," but knew that wouldn't work. Hardening her heart, she said, "Sorry,

Mark, but you're late. You remember our new rule. If you don't make it to supper on time, you have to wait until our next meal." "But, mom!" Mark pleaded, "I couldn't hear you call." "I'm sorry, Mark. You know our agreement," responded dad. Muttering under his breath, Mark left the room. It was a long time before Mark was late again! And when he was, he took it in stride. He knew he failed to arrive on time, and didn't place the blame on anyone else. Mark learned responsibility from logical consequences.

In applying logical consequences, we must be able to detach ourselves from the responsibility for our child's behavior. This is the most difficult thing to do. If Mrs. Benton had felt, "He must eat supper; it's up to me to see that he does," she could never have successfully applied logical consequences. She had to come to the point of leaving the responsibility for getting to the table entirely up to her children. If she gave in or continued to call, she would only promote continued irresponsibility. Logical consequences work only as long as we successfully remove ourselves from the power struggle and let children learn their lessons.

THE OFF-TO-SCHOOL ROUTINE

In the normal home at least one child is usually late or slow. She drags out of bed half asleep, staggers into the bathroom, has to be called to the breakfast table and barely makes it to the bus on time. If she misses the bus, she frantically runs to mother with her alert look of the day. She says excitedly, "You'll have to take me to school; I missed the bus!" The typical mother then comes to her daughter's rescue.

But what is this mother teaching her daughter? She is teaching her, "It's fine to take your time, dawdle in the bathroom, pick your way through breakfast, and miss the bus. *Mother* will solve your problem. *She* will take you to school."

Mother is rewarding her child's behavior by helping her out of a problem she created for herself.

How can this be changed? How can children learn to accept responsibility for getting off to school? In this situation we should ask ourselves, "What is the logical consequence of not getting up on time, of not getting to breakfast, and of missing the bus?" The answer is simple. The logical consequence of not getting up on time is to be late for breakfast. The logical consequence of being late for breakfast is not to eat until the next meal. The logical consequence of missing the bus is walking to school, being late, or not going to school at all!

There are only two ways to handle this every-morning problem. The first is for parents to assume responsibility. We can assume responsibility for getting our children out of bed. We can assume responsibility for getting our children to breakfast. And we can assume responsibility for getting our children to the bus on time. The responsibility is on us and the hassle remains.

The alternative is logical consequences. In this approach the child takes responsibility for his own actions. An alarm is set or we call once. When breakfast is on the table, the children are to be there. There are no second calls, no worried, "Hurry up! You'll be late!" and no more anger from parent or child. Under our old method the child resents being pushed and hurried. And we are frustrated by the slow, listless pace of a child who knows he'll be late again! Under the new method there will be no anger, since there will be no parental pressures or power struggle.

When a dawdling child misses the bus, we should not take him to school. Lateness is his responsibility, not ours. When we take him, we steal his opportunity to lear and perpetuate his immature behavior. When a child misses the bus and can walk to school safely, we should let him walk. If it is too far or too dangerous, he should stay at home. He should not be allowed to watch television or have rewarding experiences. He should stay in the house as though he were ill.

This approach causes some anxiety on the part of many mothers. How can we write a note and explain we decided not to drive Johnny to school when he missed the bus? What if a report were due, or if there were a big exam? Wouldn't that hurt his grade? That is exactly the point! If missing school hurts his grade, it is our child's responsibility, not ours. When it hurts enough, he will change his behavior to avoid negative consequences.

And what about the teacher? If it is a problem, phone her and tell her your problem and your solution. Most teachers understand and are happy to cooperate. If a teacher gets upset, your child should take that consequence. It is his fault, not yours. The displeasure of a teacher may do more to get your child to school on time than all your nagging and concern. For most children the consequences of missing school one day will be enough to solve the sleepy-eye routine. If you don't let your child take responsibility, you may face years of persistent lateness with the accompanying prodding and frustration.

SOCIAL ISOLATION AS A LOGICAL CONSEQUENCE

We have seen that most childish misbehavior reflects a search for attention, power, or revenge. Social isolation is a good way to extinguish these behaviors. Marvin was a noisy eight-year-old who turned mealtimes into chaos. He was impolite, teased his sisters, and kept up a continual chatter of upsetting, one-sided communication. Marvin's parents brought him to my office for counseling. After studying the entire family situation I suggested that Marvin be isolated during mealtimes. His mother would set up a card table in another room and allow Marvin to eat by himself. He would be told, "We love you and would like you to be with us. But we all need to relax at mealtime. If you can be quiet, you may eat with us. If you keep upsetting things, that means you would rather eat by yourself."

After I laid out this proposal Marvin's mother exclaimed, "But that would be rejecting him!" I must admit that was my initial reaction when I first saw psychologists using isolation as a means of discipline. But now I see it differently. If we say, "We don't like you. You must eat by yourself," our children will surely feel rejected. But if we let them know we love them and set up this logical consequence calmly and with sufficient warning, our children will not feel rejected. They may act as if they are to manipulate us. But they will actually profit by learning to be responsible family members. They can learn to feel accepted while acting right instead of seeking attention through negative behavior.

Sending a child to his room is another use of isolation as a logical consequence. When a child misbehaves to get attention, power, or revenge, it is logical to remove him from the place or people that cause the problem. But we must do this carefully. It we are angry and isolate a child to punish him, we only increase his anger. When we shout loudly, "Now, go to your room!" we are in a power struggle and only make matters worse. Instead, we should calmly tell our child ahead of time, "When you can't play nice, you will have to go to your room. I'm doing this to help you learn to play nicely." The first time the child misbehaves after this warning, he should be lovingly but firmly sent to his room. His isolation should have definite limits. Five minutes is usually a good beginning time. After the next offense the time may be lengthened to ten minutes. It won't be long before he learns it is better to behave and enjoy his family and friends than to misbehave and spend a half hour by himself!

The effectiveness of isolation lies in the concepts of logical consequences and extinction. When we set isolation as a loving means of discipline our children respect it as logical and fair. By removing them from people we do not reward their search for attention, power, or revenge. This lack of reinforcement will gradually cause the misbehavior to be extinguished.

SUMMARY

Natural and logical consequences are two methods of shaping your child's behavior. In natural consequences, we have only one responsibility. That is to stay out of the way and let nature run its course.

In logical consequences, we have two responsibilities. We must first structure a negative consequence that is "logically" related to the misbehavior. Then we must stay out of the way and let this consequence do our disciplining.

These methods have four advantages over those forms of discipline, such as spanking, which require direct parental intervention. First of all, *they work!* Experience is nearly always the best teacher and our children remember the lessons they learn in the school of hard knocks. *Natural and logical consequences also help avoid the power struggle.* Most family problems follow a routine cycle. The child misbehaves, the parent tries to force the child to change, and the child fights back. Natural and logical consequences avoid this cycle. The child misbehaves and suffers the consequence. Since the parent is not involved after setting the consequence, there can be no further struggle. The child's struggle is with nature or a logical consequence. It is not with his parent. Avoidance of the power struggle can relieve much of the tension in any home.

The use of logical consequences also *teaches children responsibility.* Direct parental intervention may prove the power of authority, but it doesn't teach other realities of life.

In adult life we are not spanked when we misbehave. Neither are we routinely begged or coerced into things. Instead, when we fail to do our part, we usually miss out on something good or suffer negative consequences. For example, if we fail to pay our utility bills, no one intervenes and spanks us or helps us pay the bill. Instead, we suffer the consequences and have our service discontinued! Suffering negative consequences for misbehavior is one of the best ways to help our children learn mature patterns of behavior.

The use of natural consequences also helps eliminate unnecessary nagging, corrections, and spankings. By utilizing natural and logical consequences, we substitute these commonsense ways of learning for continual parental pressure. In these four ways, natural and logical consequences can greatly improve the climate of our homes. These methods help avoid struggles for power, parental nagging, and undue physical discipline while teaching children to accept responsibility for their own behavior.

Chapter 6

TO SPANK OR NOT TO SPANK

At one time or another every parent has asked the question, "Should I spank my child or not?" Some parents mistakenly equate discipline with spanking. But, as we have seen in previous chapters, there are many ways of shaping your child's behavior. Each of these is a form of discipline. Natural consequences produce self-discipline. Your child learns through his own behavior without external interference. Spanking is at the opposite end of the continuum. As a parent, you intervene and are entirely responsible for discipline. The use of logical consequences lies somewhere in the middle. You do intervene to set the consequence of misbehavior, but your child has the option of misbehaving and enduring the consequences if he so desires. You do not force him to conform.

Each method of discipline has its advocates. But this can be very frustrating. When experts disagree, how can the average parent decide which method suits his needs? The answer is really simple. The Bible contains some very clear teachings that can guide us through the maze of conflicting theories of child training. Consider the following verses.

> And, ye fathers, provoke not your children to wrath: but bring them up in the nurture and admonition of the Lord.
> Ephesians 6:4
> He that spareth his rod hateth his son: but he that loveth him chasteneth him betimes.
> Proverbs 13:24

> Chasten thy son while there is hope, and let not thy soul spare for his crying.   Proverbs 19:18

These and other verses clearly show that God intends that parents spank their children. But this seems to contradict some of the "experts" who hold spanking in disrepute. Much of the reason for this conflict lies in the misuse of spanking. Many parents spank when they do not need to, and others severely punish children physically. This misuse of spanking is no more biblical than failing to spank at all. The biblical attitude is to spank only when necessary, and then only in love.

HOW MUCH PHYSICAL SPANKING IS NECESSARY?

We have seen the need for physical discipline and the difference between discipline and punishment. But how can we tell when to use this method? How do we know whether we are ventilating our own feelings, disciplining a child needfully, or spanking inappropriately?

We can start by asking if there is a natural or logical consequence which will teach our child the needed lesson. It is usually unwise to spank when there is another appropriate consequence available. By intervening, we may actually keep our children from learning a lesson from life. Let's take a disruptive child playing with friends, for an example. We can spank him for misbehavior. But the spanking lasts only a while and he may be willing to endure it. Since the spanking seems not to be a logical result of his misbehavior, the child may resent the discipline. Sending a child to his room would probably be a wiser choice. It is obviously related to his misbehavior. He learns that he cannot play with other children unless he plays appropriately. This use of isolation also avoids the unknowing reinforcement that some spankings bring. We have already discussed the fact that some children misbehave to get their parents' attention through spanking.

Since we should never spank a child in anger, we have another clue to physical discipline. When we are upset, we should wait until we resolve our own hostility before spanking. By then an interesting thing often happens. We usually find a more effective means of discipline!

Another guideline for physical spanking is the question, "What will most likely change his conduct?" Communication is often the best avenue of instruction, since negative behavior is your child's way of telling you something. Ten-year-old Nancy had been sulking around the house for hours. She refused to wash the dishes and seemed mad at the world! Her mother finally got the message. She said, "Nancy, you must not feel well. I'm sorry, but we all get upset once in awhile. Would you like to tell me what's bugging you?" With some reluctance, Nancy gradually began to open up. It wasn't long before she broke into a smile, and peace reigned again. Nancy was crying out to be loved and spanking would only have compounded her problem!

Younger children usually need more spankings than older ones. A one- or two-year-old child may be unable to understand adult logic and too young to suffer some hurtful natural consequences. Spankings here are certainly in order. But as a child grows, he can profit more from other types of discipline. Spanking a teenager is usually useless. It creates resentment. Spanking a two-year-old is obviously necessary at times. In the years from four to twelve, a child is usually more able to be reasoned with, to profit from natural consequences, and to have logical consequences set for other behaviors. As we increase our use of these methods, the need for spankings decreases and the power struggle is avoided.

WHY DO SPANKINGS FAIL?

Have you had the experience of repeatedly spanking your child without any change in his behavior? This can be a frustrating experience. You've tried your best, but nothing seems to work! Why do spankings sometimes fail?

When a child feels the need for more attention, he tries many ways to get it. If positive actions fail, he starts to misbehave. Take Harvey, for example. He was continually picking on his little brother. When things got really bad, Harvey's mother spanked him for hurting his little brother. But this didn't faze Harvey. Ten minutes hadn't passed before he was at it again. As long as Harvey played quietly, mother went her way. But as soon as Harvey acted up, mother dropped everything. She begged him to stop, scolded him, or warmed his little rear! But Harvey kept it up. Why? The answer is simple. Mother was reinforcing his attention-seeking behavior. By ignoring Harvey when he was good, she extinguished that behavior. By giving him attention when he misbehaved, she encouraged this reaction. *Her spankings failed to work, because she was unknowingly rewarding bad behavior.*

Inconsistency is another cause for spanking-failures. We sometimes teach our children they can get away with bad behavior. At other times, they are spanked for the same offense. Soon children realize that the law of averages is in their favor. They think, *Three out of five times I get away with this. I just got a spanking; so I should get off scot-free this time!* When the law of averages is in their favor, children take a chance. To break this, we must become consistent. If we expect consistent positive results, we must apply consistent methods.

Ineffective spankings may also be caused by insufficient pain. A mild tap for misbehavior is no deterrent for most children. They think, *Mother doesn't want me to do this, but the fun is worth a little swat. I guess I'll keep it up until it starts to hurt.* If we want to change behavior, the pain of discipline must be strong enough to outweigh the prospective enjoyment of the misdeed!

Spankings are also ineffective when used in a power struggle. When we are upset and determined to prove our authority, we set a bad example for our child. We are giving him the message: "Fight power with power." If he takes our challenge, he will be willing to suffer great pain just to prove we cannot win. When a child adopts this obstinate attitude, there is not much hope of effective discipline through spanking. We shouldn't try to outhit him or outlast him. We must use our heads. We must get out of the power struggle and find another type of motivation.

In summary, spankings may fail because of a wrong choice of disciplinary *methods,* inadequate *applications* of the method, or a poor parental *attitude.*

1. *Method:* We may have chosen the wrong form of discipline. (For example, spanking for eating soap, instead of using natural consequences.)
2. *Application:* We may be applying the method improperly. (Spanking inconsistently or too gently.)
3. *Attitude:* Our attitude may be wrong. (We may be involved in a power struggle without handling our own hostilities.)

SUMMARY

This chapter stresses the importance of proper physical discipline. The main ideas can be summarized as follows:

1. There is a place for physical discipline, but it must not be done in anger.
2. Spanking is only one type of discipline. Natural or logical consequences are other helpful methods.
3. The age of the child, the presence of natural and logical consequences, and our emotional reactions can give clues to the appropriateness of physical discipline.

Chapter 7

COMMUNICATION AS A
METHOD OF DISCIPLINE

Now we have gone over several methods of changing child behavior. These methods are reinforcement, extinction, imitation, natural consequences, logical consequences, and physical discipline. All have a valuable place in our parental role. But each has its limitations. These methods deal mainly with external behavior changes. They do little to alter our children's inner life. And this is the critical factor. The Bible says our outward actions come from the inner condition of our minds and souls. Luke 6:45 says:

> A good man out of the good treasure of his heart bringeth forth that which is good; and an evil man out of the evil treasure of his heart bringeth forth that which is evil: for of the abundance of the heart his mouth speaketh.

The experience of psychologists supports this principle. Most people with undesirable actions have inner problems which press them into bad behavior. Methods of discipline may teach good behavior and are vital to our children's personal growth. But by itself, discipline does not radically alter the personality structure. Only communication can accomplish this. Communication is essential to showing love. It is a prerequisite to gaining knowledge. To help our children grow to maturity, we must improve our communication skills.

But communication doesn't "just come naturally." There are some basic principles involved. Some have picked them up in the course of living. Most of us need special help in learning to communicate. This chapter discusses five questions that will help you evaluate your communication skills. They will give good guidelines for building better relations with your children.

DO I REALLY WANT TO LISTEN?

Have you ever rushed home with some great news only to have your mate say, "Later, honey. I'm busy just now"? Do you remember that letdown feeling? You thought, *Oh, well, I guess it wasn't that important!* Then you felt a tinge

of anger, or hurt, or rejection. The one who loved you most wouldn't take time to listen. This same thing happens to our children. When they want to talk, they need a listener. They don't want to hear, "Later, dear. Mommy's busy right now."

Does this mean we should drop everything we're doing and come running every time a child opens his mouth? Definitely not! But we should ask ourselves these questions: "What is my priority? Is this rug, dish, yard, or book as important as my relation to my son?" The answer to this question puts things in proper perspective. Most of our activities are merely physical tasks! But when we are confronted with the realities of daily duties, we often say, "My child can wait." If the dishes wait, we see the problem immediately. If the lawn waits, we notice the results in a week or two. But when a child waits, we may not see the result for years. Then we look back and wonder, "Where did I go wrong?" Children can't afford to wait!

Jesus was conducting some important business in Judaea. Hundreds were following Him and He was healing many. As He was engaged in a vital discussion with the Pharisees, some children came to visit. Jesus' disciples brushed them off. They said, "Can't you see He's busy? He has important things to do." But Jesus rebuked His mistaken disciples. He said, "Suffer little children, and forbid them not, to come unto me: for of such is the kingdom of heaven. And he laid his hands on them, and departed thence" (Matthew 19:14, 15). Jesus put the little children first!

When we are too busy to listen to our children, we are too busy. One day, as I was writing this book, my son kept interrupting. He would say, "Daddy?" But when I looked up he had nothing to say. After three or four times I realized what he was really saying. "Daddy" meant, "Daddy, will you play with me? I don't have anything to do and I want to be with you." I dropped my pen and went to the yard to play.

Then we took a ride downtown. Soon Dickie's somber mood had turned to joy. He began to sing as we rode along. We had started to communicate!

CAN I SHOW MY CHILD RESPECT?

Sam and his father were driving past a new car dealer. When Sam spotted a sharp sports car, his interest was suddenly aroused. With a ring of excitement in his voice, Sam said, "Dad, can we get a convertible next time?" "Of course not, Sam," Mr. Sloan replied sternly. "Convertibles are dangerous. Besides that, they aren't practical!" With that, the conversation ended. Sam sank down into his seat and rode on quietly. He felt a little dumb for asking such a question.

In contrast, see how this scene could have gone.

Sam. Dad, can we get a convertible next time?

Mr. Sloan. Would you like a convertible, Sam?

Sam. I think it would be great! We could drive around town with the top down and wave at our friends.

Mr. Sloan. That does sound like fun. What else do you like about convertibles?

Sam. Oh, that's about all I guess.

Mr. Sloan. Yes, that would be fun. But there are some problems, too. A convertible costs more, plus it doesn't hold the warm air as well in winter. Some people say they're not too safe. If you roll one, everyone might get crushed.

Sam. Yeah, I guess so. But it would sure be fun!

Mr. Sloan. Yes, I guess it would.

Notice the difference? Sam's question might have led to a nice little discussion. Sam would have felt good because his dad respected his idea. Sam also would have learned some things about convertibles.

But isn't this a waste of time? Wasn't it better to avoid this discussion by saying "no" and getting it over with. It all depends on our goal. If our goal is to end communication, the first approach serves the purpose. But if we want to build our child's feeling of self-worth, communicate confidence in him, and build a better relationship, taking time is very important. Children often learn their most important lessons from "unimportant discussion" like this. They learn that we respect their ideas and think they are important. These lessons are vital to their emotional development.

The High School Prom

Marilyn had just been invited to the high school prom. That evening she cornered her mother. "Mom, can I go to the prom?" Mrs. Carson quickly replied, "Of course not, dear. We've told you before. We're Christians, and Christians shouldn't dance." "But, mother," Marilyn responded, and the argument began. Let's look at a better way of handling this common problem.

Marilyn. Mother, can I go to the prom?

Mrs. Carson. Tell me about it, honey. It's coming up soon now, isn't it?

Marilyn. Yes, and Bill asked me to go.

Mrs. Carson. You kind of like him, don't you?

Marilyn. Aw, mom. I've only dated him three times.

Mrs. Carson. I know. Let's talk about the prom.

Marilyn. Well, I never get to go, and all my friends will be there.

Mrs. Carson. All your friends?

Marilyn. Well, not everyone. But our church socials are so dull!

Mrs. Carson. It seems like all the sharp kids go to the prom?

Marilyn. Not all, but most of them.

Mrs. Carson. We've talked about dancing before. . . . What do you think about Christians going to dances?

Marilyn. I don't know, mom. I know the problems — but everyone goes.

(After more discussion)

Mrs. Carson. I know you really want to go, but I just don't feel it's best to. . . .

Marilyn. But, mother. . . .

Mrs. Carson. I know, honey. But let's try to think of something to take its place. I know it won't seem as great, but we could plan something . . .

Marilyn. No! If I can't go to the prom, I don't want to do anything!

Mrs. Carson. O.K. I know how you feel.

Several lessons can be learned from this discussion. *Although Mrs. Carson had strong feelings, she respected her daughter's desires.* This is hard to do. When we feel strongly about something, we want to tell others what we think. We don't feel like listening to their opinions. Mrs. Carson knew Marilyn wouldn't agree. Nevertheless, she was willing to listen. *She was able to view things from her daughter's perspective.* She knew the church socials were dull, and she didn't try to talk Marilyn into something she didn't want. *She had also talked to Marilyn before.* The best way to avoid a crisis on issues like dancing is to talk things over as your child's interests are developing. *Mrs. Carson also controlled her feelings. She didn't get angry or try to condemn Marilyn.* She didn't imply that Marilyn was spiritually inferior because she wanted to dance. She realized this was a normal teenage wish.

When Mrs. Carson had to end the discussion, she did it in a kind way. She didn't put Marilyn down by saying, "That's just the way it is." She tried to give some valid reasons and suggest suitable alternatives. When Marilyn said she didn't want alternatives, Mrs. Carson didn't try to force one on her. That wouldn't have helped Marilyn. It would only relieve Mrs. Carson's guilt for depriving her daughter of the prom.

A New Toy

Mrs. Vernon was in the kitchen when Johnny yelled from the family room, "Mommy, can I get one of those?" (referring to the latest T.V. advertisement). "No, Johnny," Mrs. Vernon called back. "We don't have enough money. Besides, most of that stuff is junk." With a whine Johnny returned to his program. Five minutes later the scene was repeated. It would have been much better if Mrs. Vernon had handled Johnny's question like this:

Johnny. Mommy, can I get one of those?

Mrs. Vernon. You'd really like one, wouldn't you?

Johnny. Yes!

Mrs. Vernon. That would be nice. But they cost a lot of money. Mommy and daddy try to get some nice things you like, but we can't get everything you want.

Johnny. I know. (with a sigh of disgust)

Mrs. Vernon. If you really want it badly you can save your pennies and buy one.

Johnny. O.K. (knowing he won't keep his pennies that long)

Asking for toys is a little thing. But it's vitally important. The way we answer tells our children how we value their desires. While we can't buy every toy advertised, we can listen respectfully. We should avoid minimizing their wishes and their childish desires. To children, these are very real.

An Ice Cream Cone

Coming home from a late afternoon party Charlie asked, "Can we stop for an ice cream?" "Not today," his dad replied. "But I want one!" Charlie whined, threatening to break into tears. "Not today, I said!" Mr. Norton replied, his voice rising. "Please...," cried Charlie. "It will only take a minute." Having all he could take, Mr. Norton said angrily, "We're not stopping! Now, be still!"

Mr. Norton was angry and Charlie was upset. Neither profited from this exchange. Here is a better example of communication:

Charlie. Can we stop for an ice cream?

Mr. Norton. Not today, son. Mother has supper ready and we should go on home.

(Or, if he has taught his child "no ice cream before meals":)

No, son. Remember, we don't eat ice cream before supper. I'm sure mother will have a good dessert.

Charlie. But I want one! (crying)

Mr. Norton. I know. It would be nice, but we shouldn't spoil our appetites.

(Charlie continues to cry, but they are out of range of ice cream parlor and he soon stops!)

(Mr. Norton ignores the crying, since Charlie is only crying to get a response from his dad.)

Notice that Mr. Norton did not have to give in to respect Charlie's feelings. But neither did he become angry, domineering, frustrated, or authoritarian. Mr. Norton respected Charlie's wishes, explained why there would be no ice cream, reminded him of good things to come, and then ignored his crying.

In each of the previous bad examples, the parent is communicating something like this. "Your ideas or feelings are not good. We will do this my way!" The child is learning that his ideas aren't important. As this continues, a child soon feels his parents do not care. He loses self-respect and develops a poor self-image. We need to learn to respect our children while giving necessary parental guidance.

CAN I ALLOW MY CHILDREN TO EXPRESS NEGATIVE EMOTIONS WITHOUT FEAR OF RETRIBUTION?

Sandy's mother had just told her to put away her things and get ready for supper. With a glare in her eyes, Sandy shouted, "I hate you!" Upset by this apparent rejection, Mrs. Hill shot back, "Don't talk to me like that. You know better than to sass your mother!" Sandy left the room in silence but she burned inside. Let's see a better way of handling negative emotions.

Sandy. I hate you!

Mother. (In an understanding voice) You are very upset with mother.

Sandy. Yes! I want to go outside!

Mother. It makes you angry when mother won't let you go out to play.

Sandy. Yes! Can I go now?

Mother. No. (still in a quiet voice) We'll be eating in just a little while. You'd better get ready for supper now.

An angry "I hate you" is hard to take. Most of us are easily threatened. We feel our respect is being attacked and we want to fight to defend it. But when we fight back by saying, "Don't talk to me like that!" what happens? Our children actually respect us less. They know we lost our cool and tried to squelch their real emotions. By reflecting Sandy's anger, this mother helped her understand her feelings. She also showed Sandy she understood her feelings. This insight helps children develop deep respect for parents. As we respect our children's feelings, in time our children return the favor.

DO I ALLOW MYSELF TO EXPRESS POSITIVE EMOTIONS FREELY?

"Mommy! See what I made today?" yells Jimmy as he runs excitedly through the door from school. "That's terrific!" mom replies. "You did a great job! I'm glad you're doing so well in school!" With a burst of joy, Jimmy heads outside to play.

Later dad arrives. "See what I made today," Jimmy says with enthusiasm. "Let me see, son," dad replies. "That's pretty good, but you got it a little messy over here." "Yeah,

I guess I did," Jimmy sighs as he trudges off with a deflated ego.

Praise perked Jimmy up and bolstered his little ego. Criticism sent him sadly on his way. To a large extent, our children's feelings are at our mercy. By choosing to encourage them, we make life happy. By being negative and critical, we program children to become moody, hostile, or depressed.

Does this mean that we should never correct a child? Definitely not! But it does mean that we should carefully weigh the potentially damaging effect of criticism to a child's self-esteem against the improvement we hope will come through "constructive criticism." Criticism may lead to an immediate improvement of behavior. But it is also likely to lower our children's self-esteem and to cause them to withdraw from open communication. When this is true, the temporary behavior improvement is too great a price to pay.

A story is told of two young boys walking home from school. "I've carried her books twice and bought her ice cream once," the older boy said. "Do you think I ought to kiss her now?" After thinking a while, the younger boy replied, "No, I don't think you *have* to kiss her. I think you've done enough already!" The younger boy felt his friend had discharged his responsibility by carrying books and buying ice cream. He didn't think he needed to show affection, too!

Some of us are this way. As husbands, we are faithful providers. We "bring home the bacon" and are loyal fathers. But it's against our nature to be warm and complimentary. We feel awkward in showing love, or insincere when giving praise. These positive emotions just seem out of place. This difficulty in expressing positive feelings comes from our own home backgrounds. Perhaps a parent was rather cold, exacting, critical, or rigid. Growing up in that environment, we naturally adopted those feelings. Now we are passing them to another generation.

This cycle doesn't need to carry on. *We* can stop it now!
We can become positive, even though it runs against our
grain. Becoming sensitive to an overly critical spirit is the
first step. Realizing the importance of emotional support to
our children's adjustment also encourages us to grow. An
understanding mate can help us understand our feelings and
learn to express more positive emotions.

AM I OPEN TO NEW IDEAS AND WILLING TO ADMIT I AM WRONG?

Differences in opinion can develop over big and little matters. In refusing to let her fifteen-year-old daughter date,
Mrs. Marshall said firmly, "I don't think it's good. And that
settles it!" "But, mother," Diane replied, "we're going with
Wayne and Alice and we'll be home by ten o'clock." "I don't
care," Mrs. Marshall answered loudly. "When I was a girl,
we didn't date till we were sixteen. And that was early
enough." "But, mother, why can't we — just this once?" "I'm
sorry, my mind's made up," Mrs. Marshall stoutly replied.
"Now, let's forget it."

Mrs. Marshall believed she was right in protecting her
daughter. And she may have been. But did you notice her
closed mind? She was saying, "My mind's made up. Don't
confuse me with the facts." She wasn't open to another possibility. She was inflexible and didn't show respect for her
daughter's opinions. She treated Diane like an ignorant child
who had no reasonable mind of her own. This type of treatment attacks the daughter's self-esteem and promotes hostility toward the parent.

How much better it would have been if Mrs. Marshall had
been more flexible. She might have realized that things have
changed. Teenagers do date earlier. An occasional double
date could be a good experience. A mature family discussion
could do much for all the Marshalls. Sensing her mother's
respect, Diane would be more likely to uphold her confi-

dence. But being squelched by a rigid parent might cause real rebellion in a year or two.

Admitting a mistake is a difficult thing for a parent to do. We try to gain our children's respect by living up to our idea of a respectable parent. This idea usually includes being strong and intelligent. Every time we make a mistake our image takes a beating. When this happens, we can do one of two things. We can try to protect our parental image by insisting we were right, or we can be mature and admit our errors.

This is not to say we give in to all our children's whims. We are expected to be adults and have experiences our children do not have. But we must be sensitive to children's needs and thoughts. They do have many good ideas. Since we are creatures of habit, we naturally resist change. Anything new is potentially threatening. There is the subtle thought, "If we should do this differently, I must be doing it wrong now. I don't like to think I'm wrong, so I deny that things should be changed. This will protect *my* self-esteem."

But what does this attitude do to a *child's* self-esteem? He thinks he can be right only when he agrees with mom and dad. This isn't healthy. It causes a child to become a robot or a rebel. He becomes a robot if he accepts our statements. He becomes a rebel if he sees the fallacy of our logic.

Rigidity and dogmatism show themselves in little ways. Take this interchange for example:

Arnold. You said last week I could!

Mr. Sutton. (Feeling threatened) No, I didn't! Don't put words in *my* mouth!

Arnold. But, I heard you.

Mr. Sutton. I said I didn't. Now please be still!

(Conversation ends.)

Mr. Sutton defended himself and tried to prove he was right. But he did it at his child's expense. If *Mr. Sutton* was right, *Arnold* had to be wrong. Arnold either wells up in anger because he knows his father said it, or he feels stupid for "putting words in his dad's mouth." Either way he loses. Because Mr. Sutton is the parent, he wins! Because Arnold is the child, he loses. Mr. Sutton is inadvertently programming Arnold for depression or rebellion to protect his own self image.

Let's look at a better way.

Arnold. You said last week I could.

Mr. Sutton. Did I really? I don't remember saying that.

Arnold. Yes, you did. You were sitting right over there when you said it.

Mr. Sutton. (now remembering he did) Oh, that's right. Now I remember. (Or, if he still didn't think he said it:) Boy, I sure don't remember that. If I did, I'm sorry, because we just can't work it out this week.

In this way, Mr. Sutton is preserving Arnold's self-image. He isn't defending his own frail ego or calling his son a liar. Let's say Mr. Sutton really didn't make that promise. Maybe Arnold wanted it so badly he "thought" he remembered his father saying it. Or maybe he is consciously misleading his dad. By saying, "I don't remember," Mr. Sutton avoids accusing Arnold of lying. By telling Arnold he can't do it even if he promised, Mr. Sutton is extinguishing Arnold's dishonesty. Arnold will learn, "It's no use to tell dad he said something he didn't. He won't let me manipulate him that way." By handling things this way, Mr. Sutton is preserving Arnold's self-respect. He also avoids the possibility of falsely accusing Arnold because his memory failed!

Some of us find it extremely difficult to say, "I'm sorry. I was wrong." We refuse to modify our views because of children's opinions. We say piously, "Children are young and immature. They need my wisdom and guidance." But none of us are "instant parents." We are learning, too. And one of our best sources of knowledge is the children God has placed in our home. Admitting our imperfections sets a tone of mutual respect that goes a long way in promoting good parent-child relations.

HOW COMMUNICATION DISCIPLINES

Now that we have looked at the quality of our communication, let's apply these insights to child discipline. We usually think of discipline as spanking. In the first few chapters we broadened our concept of discipline. We have seen that it includes reinforcement, extinction, imitation, natural consequences, and logical consequences. Now let's take it one step farther. Good communication is another form of discipline. The basic idea can be summarized like this:

1. Misbehavior is the child's misguided effort to fill a need or gain something he wants.

2. Communication is one of the best ways to find positive means of meeting a need or seeing that a want can be discarded or delayed.

3. Therefore: If we meet a need through good communication, our children will not need to misbehave.

Other forms of discipline are largely corrective. They are "after the fact." But communication is a great preventative. When parents and children have mutual self-respect and are communicating well, many misbehaviors are avoided. Even after misdeeds occur, many are best resolved by good communication. Communication shows your child respect and leads him down the path to mature self-discipline.

Chapter 8

CHOOSING THE "RIGHT"
METHOD OF DISCIPLINE

As parents, we are all vitally concerned with shaping our children's behavior. We have discussed seven ways of doing this. But how do we know which is the appropriate method for a given problem? Some methods work in some settings, but fail in others. We need to know when to apply each plan. Although there are no "pat" answers for this, there are some principles to guide our choice of disciplinary methods. This chapter discusses guidelines for selecting the proper type of discipline.

IMITATION

One method of training requires no effort on our part. This is imitation. We use it constantly with varying results. When our behavior is appropriate, our children learn good habits. When we act out our own immaturities, our children pick these up. Above all other "methods," imitation stands alone. Our children learn most of their behavior from their parents. The single greatest gift we can give to children is our example. Other "methods" of discipline are really descriptions of good behavior for parents. They do not supercede example, they help us to fulfill it.

COMMUNICATION

Until a child understands our expectations he is in no position to respond. *This means that all discipline must begin with good communication.* Sometimes a talk is all that's necessary. On other occasions alternate methods must be used. In either case, we should always begin with communication. Our ultimate goal is self-discipline, and communication is the first step to effective self-control.

Communication may be a simple "no, no" to a ten-month-old who throws his food on the floor. But since a "no, no" is rarely sufficient for this age we should expect to follow with another method. Most ten-month-olds can't comprehend the logical consequence of not being permitted to eat if he throws food on the floor. When a child doesn't understand, removing food seems cruel. He can't comprehend why mom or dad suddenly decided to "starve" him. When this is the case, we may need to utilize physical discipline. *But,* if we spank a child's hand for throwing food on the floor without first saying "no, no" our spanking will also seem unfair. We should first give fair warning. By spanking after this verbal communication, we link "no, no" with the unpleasant consequence of spanking. This increases the likelihood that "no, no" will stop future bad behavior.

REINFORCEMENT

When you wish to strengthen good behavior the next step is *reinforcement.* A compliment, a hug, or an ice cream cone are all ways of rewarding good behavior. They each increase the chances of a repeat performance! Money is another effective reward. But it has its disadvantages. One of its disadvantages is that it comes in limited quantities! Beyond this, the underlying principles are debatable. Most of us do not want to teach our children to do everything for money. Our world has enough materialism without rearing a generation of children who feel they must be "paid" for everything they do! Some psychologists and educators advocate a point system of rewards. Children might be given fifty points for making their bed, one hundred per hour of study, twenty-five for taking out the trash and thirty for eating a complete meal. After a set number of points have been earned (let's say 5,000), the child cashes in his points for money.

Here is the problem. *The monetary reward system teaches children they "deserve" payment for routine duties.* I can't accept this as a routine plan for two reasons. For one, *it builds bad motivations.* Children should take out the trash because all family members share responsibilities, not because they're paid. Children need to learn to do their part. As adults, they won't be paid for making the bed! They will do it because it's the proper thing to do. In college mom and dad can't keep paying a dollar an hour for study time. Children should study because they want to learn or because they know they should. They should not be bribed by money.

Monetary rewards also miss the underlying problems. The reason Johnny is doing poorly in school may be a desire to get revenge on overcoercive parents. By staying out of a power struggle and letting Johnny take responsibility, his parents would solve the basic problem. But what happens when we pay Johnny for every A or B? Two things. He may get better grades. And this is good. But what about his inner attitude? If he was failing to "get a rise from mother," the money only tells him he succeeded. He improves his grades, takes the financial rewards, keeps mother in a power struggle, and loses more respect for his parents, since he knows he manipulated them into bribing him. Only by getting out of the power struggle and letting Johnny take responsibility can his parents resolve this basic problem.

Recognizing these limitations, I wouldn't ignore the important principle of reinforcement. It certainly has its place. I think the best use of financial reward is an occasional unexpected reinforcement for action above and beyond the call of duty. When a child spontaneously mows the yard or does some special task, I would sometimes give a special reward. This removes the idea of "deserving to be paid" and the bad motivation connected with it. Money then becomes a special bonus for special occasions.

There is also a place for monetary reinforcement procedures with emotionally disturbed children. But this is a limited group and their treatment schedule should be used only on prescription from trained professional personnel.

EXTINCTION

When you want to weaken negative behavior, you should always utilize extinction. Find the reward your child is gaining from bad behavior and see that it is stopped. Is he seeking attention, fighting for power, attempting to build his sense of worth, looking for revenge, or searching for psychological safety? Finding his motivation and removing the reward is the first step in extinguishing that negative behavior.

NATURAL CONSEQUENCES

If communication hasn't been effective, you can turn to natural consequences. This method is effective for any behavior that has unpleasant results. Of course, natural consequences can't be used if they will cause severe harm to your child. But this is a delicate point. We are often squeamish about natural consequences because of our own anxiety and guilt. We hate to see our children suffer. We think, "I can't let *that* happen to my child." So we intervene. However, we shouldn't allow our fears to keep us from doing the right thing for our children. A little physical pain is much better for children than repeated naggings, spankings, and power struggles. The temporary pain of natural consequences is a great preventative for years of unhappiness. It is nearly always more effective than all the talking and spanking we can muster!

LOGICAL CONSEQUENCES

Logical consequences should also be reserved until verbal communications have failed. When no natural consequences exist, or when the natural consequences would cause severe hurt, we should rely on logical consequences. This method helps avoid the power struggle and aids children in developing a sense of responsibility and self-discipline.

PHYSICAL DISCIPLINE

Spanking should be our last resort. All other methods encourage growth toward self-discipline. This is essential to emotional maturity. Spankings make children dependent on others for direction. Although spankings are sometimes necessary we should remember they do not promote *self-discipline*. This limits their effectiveness. God uses physical pain to teach His sons some lessons. And we should do the same. But we should reserve this method for times when other plans have failed. The following table summarizes the information on selecting the appropriate form of discipline.

Table 2

CHOOSING A METHOD OF DISCIPLINE

Method of Discipline	When to Use	Lesson the Child Learns
COMMUNICATION	1. In all cases. 2. Before any other methods are tried.	"By talking, I see the advantages and disadvantages of my planned action. Therefore, I will willingly do the proper thing. My parents respect me and I think they have good ideas."
REINFORCEMENT	Any time you want to strengthen a desirable behavior.	"When I do the desirable thing, I get rewarded for it. Therefore, I will do it again."
EXTINCTION	Any time you want to weaken undesirable behavior.	"When I behave undesirably, I do not get any reward. Therefore, there is no sense in doing that again."

Method of Discipline	When to Use	Lesson the Child Learns
NATURAL CONSEQUENCES	1. When you want to weaken undesirable behavior. 2. When communication and extinction have not worked.	"When I do some things I get hurt. Nobody else has anything to do with it. I just bring on a bad experience. Therefore, I will not do that again."
LOGICAL CONSEQUENCES	1. When you want to weaken undesirable behavior. 2. When communication and extinction have not worked. 3. When no natural consequence exists. 4. When natural consequences would cause severe or lasting hurt to the child.	"The world has many people. When I do something that is wrong, they may impose some undesirable consequences. Therefore, I will do my part in order to avoid the negative consequences."
PHYSICAL SPANKING	When all other methods have failed	"My parents are my authority. They have the experience to know what is right and to enforce their guidelines by inflicting physical pain. Though I do not like it at the time, I am learning it is for my good and they do it because they love me."
IMITATION	This method is in continuous operation.	"My parents are strong and grown-up. Since they act that way, so should I."

PART 3

Your Child's Inner Life

Personal adjustment involves both external behaviors and internal emotions. To be successful parents we must help our children in both of these areas. Proper actions in an unhappy child are of little value. On the other hand, a "happy" child with repeated misbehavior is likewise undesirable. Part 3 discusses the child's self-image. Chapter 9 summarizes the basic elements of the child's image. Chapter 10 shows how to meet these needs. Our success in building our children's self-esteem will largely determine their inner peace.

Chapter 9

SELF-IMAGE: THE KEY
TO YOUR CHILD'S ADJUSTMENT

I once asked a woman counselee to finish ten times the sentence "I am . . . ." Slowly and hesitantly, she replied:
"I am a poor mother."
"I am overweight."
"I am unhappy."
"I am a disappointment to my parents."
"I am divorced."
"I am lonely."
At that point I gently interrupted and said, "I didn't ask you to say ten bad things about yourself. Try again and finish it with good statements." "No, I can't," she said with discouragement. "Sure you can," I encouraged. "No," she said, breaking into tears. "I can't think of anything good to say." After some more prodding, she reluctantly said, "I try to be a good mother." Later she said, "I try to keep a clean house." This was all the good she could muster up about herself. She felt she was a complete failure. She thought her life was worthless.

Another client, the thirty-two-year-old wife of a minister, was relating her personal problems. At the end of our first session, she blurted out in despair, "I'm no good! I'm no

good! I'm no good! I'm supposed to be a minister's wife, and
look how bad I am!" The young divorcee and the minister's
wife were suffering from similar problems. They were both
depressed and had very poor self-concepts.

Each of us has a self-concept or self-image. We have
learned to think of ourselves in certain ways. Sometimes
this image is good. Sometimes it is bad. Many psychologists
see this self-image as the key to personal adjustment. If we
have a good self-image, we are considered "adjusted." If we
think poorly of ourselves, we are considered "maladjusted."

Throughout this book we have been looking at ways of
shaping our children's behavior. This is a parent's most obvious task. When a child misbehaves, we see results immediately. But overt behavior is only one aspect of rearing children. There is another, deeper level. This is the inner area
of your child's self-esteem.

All of our behavior is guided by our self-esteem. When a
child thinks he is a "bad" boy, he will probably act that way.
When he thinks he is a "good" boy, he will live up to that
image. Sometimes we get the opposite effect. A child who
inwardly believes he is a "bad" person may try to overcome
this feeling by good behavior. By changing his behavior, he
thinks he will change his feelings about himself. But this
usually doesn't work.

I once talked with the president of a large corporation. He
was extremely successful financially and a fine gentleman.
Active in his church, he had a good Christian witness. His
home life was good and he seemed to "have it made." From
all outward appearances, he should have a good self-image.
You would think this man was confident and happy. But his
inner feelings were another story. Telling of his deep depression, he said, "Sometimes I feel a complete failure. Life
doesn't seem worth living. I guess I know I'm a success, but
I sure don't feel that way inside." No amount of reassurance

could convince this man to like himself. As a boy he had developed a poor self-image. Try as he might, he could never please his father. He always had to be the best. Anything short of this was failure. He began to think, "I can never do well enough to please." But he didn't give up. He earned excellent grades in school and did well in high school sports. He kept on striving until he became a millionaire. He thought this would surely satisfy his needs. But even then he wasn't happy. He was unable to accept himself because of a poor self-image.

Our self-concepts are shaped in early life and resist great changes later on. We value ourselves more by this inner sense of worth than by our adult accomplishments. This is one of the greatest paradoxes of life. Many outwardly successful people are depressed and anxious because of poor self-images developed during childhood.

Our child's feelings about himself, his self-image, will largely determine his happiness in life. If he learns to accept himself and his abilities, he can handle life effectively. If he develops a negative self-image, he may struggle through life with feelings of depression, anxiety, guilt, or anger. It is not enough to shape our child's behavior. We must also help him develop proper self-esteem. This self-image has three main features. They are a sense of confidence, a sense of belonging, and a sense of worth.

A SENSE OF BELONGING

When my counselee finished her sentence with statements like, "I am lonely," "I am divorced," and "I am unhappy," she was reflecting a deep sense of loneliness. She felt alone, rejected, and depressed. She had lost her husband and disappointed her parents. She had nowhere to turn. She felt she didn't belong! A sense of belonging is a universal need. We all crave love and affection. We want to be needed. We want others to care. Children are no exception. Perhaps

their greatest need is the need for a sense of belonging. This
is the first ingredient in a healthy self-image. All children
need to feel they are in an atmosphere of affection and
love.

But doesn't every parent love his children? Of course,
with rare exceptions. But there is sometimes a big gap between a parent's love and a child's perception of it. It is not
sufficient to say, "I love my children" and let it go at that.
*We must become sensitive to how our children are under-
standing our love.* This calls for careful thought and action.

A SENSE OF WORTH

When the minister's wife blurted out, "I'm no good! I'm
no good! I'm no good!" she was expressing a deep sense of
worthlessness. She felt she was such a bad person that no
one could love her. This attitude led to a sense of worthlessness. Her judgment of herself was wholly unwarranted, both
in view of her own high Christian principles and in view of
the grace of God.

Yet her mistake is a common one. Early in life children
learn that others are constantly evaluating their performance.
When these evaluations are genuinely good, the child develops a healthy self-esteem. When the evaluations are con-
sistently negative, he develops a feeling of "badness." This
"badness" is basic to adult feelings of depression. The depressed person feels he is no good. He prays, but God doesn't
seem to hear. Since he imagines he's such a "bad" person,
he can't accept forgiveness. Time after time he cries for forgiveness, only to get a temporary reprieve from his harsh
self-condemnations. Early parental evaluations are at the
base of these neurotic feelings. On the other hand, a good
sense of self-esteem results from proper parental care. As
parents, we have a great opportunity to instill in our children
a healthy sense of value and of worth.

A SENSE OF CONFIDENCE

Some years ago I had the experience of testing four-year-old children who were applying for kindergarten. One morning little Ruthie came to my office. I said cheerfully, "Hi, Ruthie! How are you this morning?" "Waah," she cried, as she clung to her mother's skirt. "Have you seen our fish?" I asked, trying to win her favor. "Waah," she cried again as she held tightly to her mother. "Would you like to play some games?" I asked, using all the psychology I could muster. But still she clung to her mother. Try as I might, I couldn't get her away from mother. She was scared stiff. She had no confidence.

An hour or so later little Billy arrived. "Hi," I said. "How are you this morning?" "Fine," Billy enthusiastically replied; "how are you?" "Great," I answered. "Have you seen our fish?" "Yes, we have some at home," Billy said alertly. "Let's play some games," I said. "Good!" Billy replied as he walked confidently into my office.

What a contrast! At four years of age Billy was a sharp, confident little guy. Ruthie was already heading for problems. *The difference was in their self-esteem.* Billy liked himself and felt a sense of confidence. Ruthie was afraid of people and lacking in confidence.

I thought to myself, *What will these kids be like in a few years?* When speech class rolls around, Ruthie will be in trouble. She will be tense, nervous, and upset. Billy will have no problem. It they join a church, their personalities will continue to show. Billy could be the chairman of a visitation committee. Ruthie would be scared to death to knock on a door. These traits are well established by the age of six or eight. And they are difficult to change. This is not to say the self-esteem can't be altered. It can. But once a basic personality pattern is set, it takes careful parental planning to help a child develop most positive self-evaluations.

Chapter 10

BUILDING YOUR CHILD'S SELF-IMAGE

A child's self-image is very pliable. During the first few years of life, we can shape it any way we want. If we want a child to be depressed and feel unworthy, we can achieve that. All it takes is a steady diet of low value judgments. We can tell him, "You're a bad child"; "You're naughty," and "You're no good." Soon he will believe our evaluations and incorporate them into his self-esteem. He will think, *I am a bad child.*

On the other hand, we can make a child feel his immense worth by showing him our unconditional love. This means we accept our children fully, no matter how they act. When children disobey, we discipline, but we shouldn't attack their character. We may say, "That is wrong"; "You are not to do that," or "That's a bad thing to do." But we shouldn't say, "You are bad," or, "You're a dirty child." We should focus on the misdeed, not on our children's sense of worth. In this way we teach them right and wrong while maintaining their self-esteem.

This chapter discusses several effective ways of building your child's self-esteem.

BUILDING SECURITY AND CONFIDENCE BY ESTABLISHING NECESSARY RULES

Children are impulsive and immature. They need parental guidance to function well and feel secure. The Bible makes it clear that we should set limits on our children's actions. In 1 Samuel, Eli is rebuked for failing to restrain his sons. He knew of their misdeeds but failed to restrain them. [1] In this age of permissiveness we should be careful to establish needed guidelines for our children.

But these guidelines should be carefully established. A teenager asks, "Why can't I?" and a mother replies, "Because I said so!" This isn't healthy. We shouldn't set rules on the basis of our whims, habits, or personal biases. As parents, we should sit down and logically establish necessary rules for our children's protection. Since having too many rules is frustrating, we should also see what rules can be eliminated.

When our son was just a toddler, we had a nice vase setting on a camphor chest in the living room. The vase interested Dickie immensely. In spite of our warnings and a few swats on the hand, he continued to make his way to that corner of the room. Finally we wised-up. We put the vase on a higher shelf. This immediately solved our problem. We had been tempting Dickie unnecessarily. There were plenty of "no, no's" to teach him obedience without chancing a broken vase. So we "kiddie-proofed" our home.

We should avoid unnecessary regulations since imposing too many restrictions may cause problems. No one likes to have someone continually saying, "You can't do this," or, "You can't do that." Constant restriction upsets us all. When many rules are set, some children become discouraged. They feel they can never meet all the rules so they give up. As this pattern continues, they grow nervous and depressed.

Other children have an opposite reaction. They decide to rebel. Since they are tired of trying, they throw off all parental guidelines and "live it up." To avoid this, we should limit our regulations to only those that are essential. This

[1] 1 Samuel 3:13, "For I have told him that I will judge his house for ever for the iniquity which he knoweth; because his sons made themselves vile, and he restrained them not."

gives needed security but avoids a feeling of failure or a need
to rebel.

BUILDING A SENSE OF BELONGING BY
EXPLAINING REASONS FOR RULES

"Because I said so!" is one of the worst things a parent can
say. It tells a child, "You aren't important enough to get an
answer." It tears at their self-respect and tells them they
aren't wanted. Sometimes we are threatened by our children's questions and try to turn them off with a final, "Just
because!" That may end the conversation. But it's damaging to our children's self-image. Children have a hard time
feeling they belong when they aren't even deserving of a
good explanation. If we want our children to feel our love,
we must be willing to communicate. This doesn't mean we
give a detailed answer to every off-hand "Why?" But it does
mean we respect our child's right to an honest answer when
he asks an honest question. This promotes both a sense of
worth and a feeling of belonging.

PROMOTING A SENSE OF BELONGING BY
FINDING A SUBSTITUTE ACTIVITY

Mrs. Abbot had just discovered her two-year-old playing
with her china. "Honey, you shouldn't play with mother's
china. Here's your own dish. Let's see what you can do with
it." Mrs. Abbot recognized an important principle. Every
time we deprive children of an object or activity, we should
try to give them something in its place.

Think how some days go for a child. "Turn off the record
player, son. It's too loud." "Don't play in that room. Mother
just cleaned it." "Don't get into that. I don't have time to
pick up after you today." And on it goes. At every turn the
child meets frustration. It seems as if mother is trying to deprive him. She isn't, of course, but it surely seems that way.
The continual frustration of his wishes soon discourages the

child. He feels mother doesn't care to make him happy. He begins to feel unloved and his self-image is affected. He values himself this way: "My parents never let me have any fun. They must not care for me. I really don't belong."

In contrast to a pattern of deprivation is God's dealing with His children. The Bible certainly has its "no, no's." But in their place God gives an exciting life of challenge and contentment. Some Christians have trouble believing this. They see God as a stern Father who wants to deprive them of fun and fulfillment. They live by a set of "no, no's," and their Christian experience is one of suffering and defeat. They can't look at the positive side. One such woman told me, "I can't believe God wants me to be happy. Every time I have some fun I feel a little guilty. It seems like I must be wasting time and that I should be working." This pattern of thinking is learned in childhood from parents who are punitive or who fail to give enough enjoyable experiences to their children.

We need to plan for our children's playtime. Boredom and misbehavior are usually signs that a child doesn't have enough to do. When we see these signs, we should take stock of our child's recreational facilities. Although television has its disadvantages, selected programs can be good for children. An hour or two of T.V. is entertaining to a child. Some programs also have an educational value. The hour or two of uninterrupted time is also a boon to busy mothers! We shouldn't apologize for this. Parents are people, too. We need time alone in the midst of busy days. By keeping children busy we not only help their growth, we maintain our peace of mind. This isn't to say we turn on the T.V. each morning and forget the kids till night! Children need supervision in selecting programs. They also need personal attention and a variety of activities. But television is one potentially good activity for children.

Outdoor play areas are essential. With increased urban living many children don't have sufficient body exercise. When little bodies are tense, problems are likely to arise. Tempers flare and mischief increases. A sand box, a swing set, and a free play area help relieve pent-up emotions. By discharging these feelings in active play, they no longer erupt in misbehavior.

The Bentons were having trouble with their pre-school boy. For a few weeks, Vernon had become increasingly irritable and moody. There were no particular problems in the family, and they couldn't explain his sudden surge of misbehavior. Vernon would wander around the house just "looking for trouble." Finally, they concluded that he was bored. The Bentons had a small yard, but it was landscaped nicely. They didn't want the kids to mess it up. But after talking things over, they decided to sacrifice a corner of the yard. They purchased a small swing set and Mr. Benton built a sandbox out of bricks. Within a day, they noticed a change. Vernon spent a good deal of his time in the yard. And when he came inside, he seemed less tense. He was more relaxed and happy. The swing set cost a little money and the grass in the corner of the yard took a beating, but it was a good investment. Vernon knew his parents loved him. They had sensed his boredom and frustration and had found some stimulating things for him to do.

But keeping children busy is not a one-time task. Children's interests change. We need to remain sensitive to the experiences which hold their interests and meet their current needs.

BUILDING CONFIDENCE THROUGH PRAISE

A newly married client was relating her tremendous lack of self-confidence. "I'm such a poor wife," she said. "I don't keep the house clean and I don't deserve a husband like Don." As she continued to relate her lack of confidence in her role as a wife, she told this story. "My father was very hard to please. I couldn't seem to do anything right. One day he was out working and my mother was gone. I knew daddy loved chocolate cake. I took all morning and made him the nicest cake I could. I was so excited! I knew he would be so happy! Finally he came home. When he saw the cake, he said, 'Who made that?' 'I did!' I said proudly. With that, he took the cake and threw it in the sink. He said in anger, 'I never want to eat anything you make!' She sobbed as she related this story. It was obvious that much of her present problem came from that type of experience. Perhaps unconsciously, her father had succeeded in smashing her self-image through continued ridicule and criticism.

Few parents have such extreme problems as this man. But we can subtly tear at the foundation of our children's self-esteem. *Every criticism is a blow to a child's self-image. Each compliment helps to build an inner sense of confidence.* We often unwittingly tear down our children's self-image by what we think is "constructive criticism." We are sincerely interested in our child's performance. We want him to do well. So we point out his errors. We say, "That was good, Andy, but you could have done a little better." We mean to help. But what runs through Andy's little mind? He thinks, *I can't do very well. Daddy said I did it well, but he really didn't like it.* Andy is developing a poor self-image. As an adult, he will be an anxious person with little confidence.

No parent consciously wants to destroy his child's self-confidence. But many do it just the same. Why is it that sincere, loving parents are over-critical with children? The basic reason lies in the parent's own self-image. We have strong needs to feel proud of ourselves and our children. We want to believe we are "good" parents. Naturally, our children are the key to our parental self-images. A well-mannered, intelligent, achieving child is a feather in our cap. An "average" child with "so-so" school performance does little to boost our parental egos! So we try to improve their behavior. Criticism is one of our major weapons.

If we make a child feel, "I am not doing well," we think he will improve. And he may, but a couple of negative things may happen, too. Since he feels he isn't doing well, he may give up entirely. He feels, "Since I can't do anything right, what's the use of trying?" In this case, parental criticism only makes things worse. Other children do respond to criticism. They think, "I'm not doing well, and my parents aren't pleased with me. I'll do better so they'll be happier with me." In this case, we get improved behavior. But what about the self-image? His ego takes a beating. He thinks we don't love him unless he achieves to our satisfaction. We sacrifice the long-range goal of a good self-image for the present satisfaction of a high-quality performance. This is not a good decision. *It is more important for a child to develop wholesome attitudes than ideal behavior.* A well-adjusted person with a good self-image will perform well in time. Good behavior will flow from good feelings. But the opposite is not true. Once a poor self-image develops, even perfect performance will not erase the nagging doubts of self-esteem.

I often tell parents it takes about one hundred compliments to make up for one criticism. I'm not sure of the exact ratio. But I do know this: children are sensitive and easily discouraged. We need to support, encourage, and compliment them freely. We should keep criticisms to the bare minimum to protect our children's self-esteem.

BUILDING A SENSE OF WORTH BY SHOWING RESPECT

The story is told of a family that went out to dinner. The waitress said to the young boy, "What would you like to eat, sonny?" "I'll have a hamburger," Henry proudly announced. Interrupting, his mother "maturely" said, "He'll have roast beef!" "And what would you like on your hamburger?" the waitress asked. "I'll have mustard and ketchup," Henry replied. With a stern look, Henry's mother said, "He'll have some green beans!" Ignoring the mother, the waitress continued, "And what would you like to drink?" Henry answered, "I'll have a coke!" With her motherly look, Mrs. Hansen sternly said, "He'll have some milk!" The waitress left. Soon she returned with exactly what Henry ordered. With a sense of amazement, Henry turned to his mother and said, "Gee, mom. She thinks I'm real!"

Sometimes we are like this mother. We imply, "Adults are important people. You children are fine and we love you. But when you get big, you'll be more important."

In great contrast to this is the value God places on children. God made man as the crowning glory of His creation. He judged man to be of such value that He sent His Son to purchase us from sin. And Jesus clearly showed the value of children when He said, "Suffer little children, and forbid them not, to come unto me: for of such is the kingdom of heaven . . ." (Matthew 19:14). God places a great value on every person and it is our responsibility to give our children a glimpse of that eternal worth. *By treating our children as valuable people, we do much to lay the foundation for a healthy self-image.*

DESTROYING A SENSE OF WORTH BY GUILT MOTIVATION

"Martha! Don't you feel ashamed of yourself? Look at all we've done for you and now you treat us that way!" Martha's parents are trying to make her feel guilty so she will do what they want. This is a horrible way to motivate a child! In trying to produce good behavior, Martha's parents are lowering her self-esteem. They are making her feel, "I'm ungrateful. I'm unthoughtful. I'm no good." These feelings cause depression, discouragement, and despair.

We sometimes think, "If I can make her feel bad enough, maybe she will change." True, she may! But what about her feelings? Martha may be thrown into a pattern of depression and self-condemnation because she is developing a feeling of worthlessness. We must continually ask ourselves, "Will the method I'm choosing to change my child's behavior build his sense of self-esteem?"

Using adjectives like "bad," "no good," and "dirty" is another unthinking way of destroying a child's feeling of worth. You know how *we* react to these evaluations. They depress us — or they make us angry. Our children are no different. They are very sensitive to negative evaluations.

A sense of worthlessness needs to be distinguished from a lack of righteousness and the presence of sin. We shouldn't teach our children they can do no wrong. Instead, we should tell them of God's holiness and justice. Through Bible stories, prayers, and talking, we can help our children see God's holy standards and their need of salvation.

But we shouldn't use guilt as a club to force good behavior. The purpose of teaching children about sin and holiness is to show God's righteous standards and lead a child to Christ, God's answer to the problem.

We often distort this biblical teaching on sin to force our children into good behavior. We think they will change if we make them feel bad enough. But this is wrong. The Holy Spirit convicts of sin. And we should teach our children right and wrong. But we can do this without making them feel "no good" or "useless." Motivation by guilt causes one of two reactions. Some children behave correctly but develop feelings of depression. Others react to guilt motivations by turning to bad behavior. They think, *Since my parents think I'm bad, I may as well behave that way.*

But how can we teach about sin without attacking our children's sense of worth? We cannot allow children to ignore their sinful behavior. But neither should we destroy their self-esteem. We must maintain a healthy balance. A proper teaching on sin should include the following five elements:

1. It should teach God's standards of holy living. (Galatians 5:19-26)
2. It should show a child how we all fall short of these standards. (Romans 3:23)
3. It should show a child how valuable he is to God and distinguish between one's being a sinner and being a worthless person. (1 Corinthians 1:1-9)
4. It should lead the child to Christ, the answer to his sin. (John 3:16; 1:12)

5. It should encourage the child to be obedient out of the motivation of love, not of guilt. (Ephesians 5:1, 2; 1 John 4:11-18)

When a child realizes that God created him and that Christ died for him, he gains a new vision of his worth. With this self-esteem, he is in a good position to acknowledge his sinful behavior and to be willing to change. He doesn't have to sacrifice a sense of his own value to admit his sinful behavior.

TEACHING CONFIDENCE AND A SENSE OF BELONGING BY GIVING RESPONSIBILITY

Everyone needs to feel important. We want to feel we have a place. By giving children responsibilities, we build their self-esteem. If Marty takes out the trash each day, he feels important. He thinks, "Mother cooks, daddy goes to the office, and I take out the trash. We each do important things!" This is good for his self-concept. Marty comes to see himself in a good light and also learns to do his part. This doesn't mean he will always enjoy taking out the trash. As a matter of fact, he may often "forget," or "refuse." But these lapses are a way of testing his parents. He knows it would be easier to forget the trash, so he gives it a try. If his parents become angry and try to force him, Marty responds with greater resistance. But when his parents calmly say, "We each have important things to do, Marty," and set a logical consequence (such as no trash, no supper), Marty will respond favorably. He doesn't want his parents to lord it over him, but he does gain an inner sense of fulfillment by carrying his share of the load.

BUILDING CONFIDENCE BY PROMOTING INDIVIDUALITY

A newborn baby is totally dependent. Without parents or parent-substitutes, he cannot continue to exist. At some time around the age of twenty we all reach adulthood. At that time we are to stand on our own two feet. We should be able to earn a living, care for ourselves, leave our parents, and start our own life. During the period from birth to twenty our children need to gradually gain a feeling of self-identity and independence. The two-year-old is not as needy as the infant. But he is still dependent. Most seventeen-year-olds have developed a strong sense of autonomy. But they are not entirely free of their need for parental guidance and support.

Children must be steadily growing toward a sense of autonomy and independent identity if they are to build a healthy self-image. We are the key to this struggle. By encouraging independent thoughts and actions, we promote a sense of confidence and strength. By overprotecting or squelching a child, we undermine his confidence. This makes it harder for him to cope with adult life.

Some time ago my wife and I visited the home of some very "conservative" friends. As soon as we entered the kitchen we were struck by something new. The kitchen had been papered with a bright, "hippie-type" paper! Immediately we surmised what had happened. Teri, the teenage daughter, saw the wallpaper in a store. She said, "Mom, couldn't we?" Mother was somewhat hesitant, knowing her husband's strong desires for traditional tastes. But she decided to give it a try. Finally she convinced her husband no harm would come.

We checked our hunches and found we were right. I thought to myself, *Isn't that good! These parents respect their daughter's opinions and treat her as an intelligent person. She won't have to rebel later in life to "find herself." She is already gaining a healthy sense of identity by being treated with respect.*

The failure to let children gradually mature is one of the greatest causes of teenage rebellion in Christian homes. Because we are God's representatives, we sometimes try to play God to our children. *We* set all the standards. *We* make all the decisions. And *we* let children know their place. Each of these parent behaviors undermines a child's identity. He begins to wonder if he can do anything on his own. And he resents being "treated like a child." Gradually resentment builds. But the child is afraid to assert himself against a strong authoritarian parent. He continues to suppress his feelings. Finally something happens. He either leaves home and starts to rebel or keeps his feelings in and becomes depressed. The wise parent senses his child's needs for independence and self-esteem and does everything possible to promote these healthy attitudes.

SUMMARY

Our children's life adjustment can be understood in terms of self-esteem. To the degree they lack self-esteem, they will suffer problems. We are the key to our children's self-esteem. When we stifle them through criticism, guilt motivation, unrealistic regulations, and overprotection, we program our children for lives of failure and frustration. When we encourage, guide, and support them, we help build healthy attitudes which last a lifetime.

PART 4

Parents Are People, Too

Most of us have a fair idea of how our children should be treated. But that is not enough. The real difficulty comes in applying what we know. It is one thing to realize the dangers of our anger. It is another thing to keep our cool when our child has just broken a favorite vase or practiced his alphabet on the hallway wall.

This section deals with the negative parental emotions of anger, fear, and guilt. This trio of feelings can easily derail our best-laid plans for effective relations between parent and child. By playing on these emotions, our children often manipulate us at will. They provoke us to anger, they make us feel cruel when we discipline, and they manipulate us into choosing sides in sibling conflicts because we are afraid.

Negative emotions also cause us much parental anguish. They tear at our peace of mind and upset our emotional health. To live happy lives and rear our children well, we must learn to handle our emotions.

Chapter 11

LOSING YOUR COOL

"I want to sit up there," said Billy as Mrs. Thomas and her three children climbed into the car for a trip downtown. "Not today, Billy," replied Mrs. Thomas. "Sharon is already in the front seat." "But I want to!" whined Billy a little louder. "Not today!" said mother, her voice rising. "Now let's go!" Billy shoved his sister and began to cry loudly. "Billy, be quiet!" yelled Mrs. Thomas, to no avail. And that was the beginning. The whole morning ran that way. At the slightest disappointment, Billy broke into tears. Soon everyone's nerves were on edge. During the morning Billy received three hard swats, ten threats of spankings, and a dozen or so pleadings to good behavior. When they finally returned home around noon Mrs. Thomas was a wreck. She thought to herself, "I can *never* get anything done when those kids are around!"

Mrs. Thomas was frustrated. She had her morning planned and Billy upset the applecart. Let's see what happened.

1. Mrs. Thomas had a plan for the morning (shopping, the cleaners, and a quick visit to drop some things at a friend's home).
2. Billy had a plan (to ride in the front seat and get his way all morning).
3. Sharon had a plan (to sit by mother and get attention by being good).
4. Sharon's plan upset Billy's and made him angry.

5. Billy's plan upset mother and made her angry.

6. Mrs. Thomas' anger gave Billy more attention, and that fit nicely into his plan.

7. Now Billy and Sharon were both operating according to plan. (Sharon was getting attention in a positive way and Billy in a negative way.)

8. Mrs. Thomas was the only one not operating according to plan!

9. Being frustrated and needing some peace and quiet, Mrs. Thomas tried to change Billy's behavior by yelling and spanking.

10. Since Billy was determined to get attention any way he could, Mrs. Thomas was actually rewarding his crying and making it more likely to happen again!

What could Mrs. Thomas do to avoid this power struggle? The principle is simple. She could refuse to become angry, thus sidestepping a power struggle. Then she could quietly tell Billy they would not leave the driveway until he became quiet. She would then sit calmly and wait. After this happened a time or two, Billy would learn that crying spells are not a good way of getting attention from mother.

The same principle is true downtown. Billy should either be sent to the car or told to wait in a safe part of the store if he is old enough. If these methods would be dangerous, Billy should be warned once that he will not go shopping with mother next week if he cries again. If he does cry, Mrs. Thomas *must* follow through with the logical consequence of not allowing Billy to go shopping next time. This method will cause you a little trouble and a few dollars for a baby-sitter. But look at what is gained. Your weekly shopping trips can become a pleasant experience instead of a harried hassle! All you have to do is apply the logical consequences of not starting the car until order reigns and not taking Billy shopping if he continues to be disruptive.

Most childish misbehavior in the car can be handled the same way. Instead of fraying your nerves and losing your cool, simply pull to the side of the road and wait. But your attitude must also be right. You can't do this effectively if you silently communicate, "*I* will show *you!* This car isn't *budging* until everyone shuts up!" With this attitude, you are still in a power struggle because of your own anger. You must first resolve your feelings. Then you can effectively pull to the side of the road and calmly say, "It is difficult to drive when children are fighting and yelling. When you can stop, we will go on." You don't need to threaten to stop the car. This only makes things worse. Tell your children the consequence ahead of time and quietly stop during the first offense.

This sounds easy, but few parents use this simple and effective method. Why is that? We have a sure way of changing behavior but continue to nag, threaten, and suffer turmoil instead of using this proven means. The problem lies in our attitudes! Pulling off the freeway seems like an inconvenience. We think stubbornly, "*We* are the parents. *We* should not have to stop for screaming kids. Let *them* shape up!" So what happens? The kids respond to our challenge of authority. They think, "*We'll* show them who's boss! *We* will cause such a commotion they will become angry. In this way *we* will have the satisfaction of winning the war. *We may lose the battle* (by eventually quieting down). *But we will win the war* (by frustrating our parents)."

I realize we can't always pull off the highway immediately. We may need to change lanes gradually or find a freeway exit. This does cause inconvenience. And maybe parents *shouldn't* have to inconvenience themselves. But the point is this. Once reason fails to work, stopping the car is the only effective method of discipline. Spankings and threats only continue the power struggle. Besides, isn't the temporary inconvenience of pulling off the road a few times worth a lifetime of peaceful car riding? Sometimes we want our children's behavior to change but are unwilling to apply an appropriate method of discipline. Then we blame our children for not responding to our own immature threats and tantrums. How much better to take time to calmly use a really effective method of child training.

Let's take a closer look at our feelings of anger and frustration. These emotions are really identical. Since anger is bad, we often refuse to admit we are angry or hostile. Instead, we say naively, "No, I'm just frustrated!" What we really mean is, "I'm angry, but I don't like to recognize it or admit it."

Anger comes in many forms. It can show up in a harsh

word, a raised voice, a hard spanking, a cutting sense of humor, or a passive withdrawal. Some parents become aggressive and attack when they are angry. Others retreat under the influence of negative emotions.

Anger is destructive. It tears at family unity and also hurts the angry one. No one profits from this universally negative emotion. But it is not easily put away. Let's look at the dynamics of hostility and some ways of resolving it.

The Bible sheds vital light on the problem of hostility. Our starting place is overcoming the notion that hostility is harmless. We like to think we deserve to be angry when things go wrong. This is a natural feeling. But it is not biblical. And it is not healthy. It is natural to become angry, but it isn't good. We can never discipline effectively until we resolve our hostile feelings. We may get conformity out of fear. But we can't build healthy emotional responses in our children by utilizing anger. The following passages clearly show that hostile emotions arise from our carnal nature (italics mine):

> Dear brothers, don't ever forget that it is best to listen much, speak little, and not become angry: *for anger doesn't make us good, as God demands that we must be.* So get rid of all that is wrong in your life, both inside and outside.
>
> James 1:19-21a (*The Living Bible*)

> But when you follow your own wrong inclinations your lives will produce these evil results: impure thoughts, eagerness for lustful pleasure, idolatry, spiritism (that is, encouraging the activity of demons), *hatred* and *fighting,* and *anger,* constant effort to get the best for yourself, *complaints* and *criticisms,* the feeling that everyone else is wrong except those in your own little group — and there will be wrong doctrine, envy, murder, drunkenness, wild parties, and all that sort of thing. Let me tell you again as I have before, that anyone living that sort of life will not inherit the kingdom of God.   Galatians 5:19-21 (*The Living Bible*)

Stop your anger! Turn off your wrath. Don't fret and worry
— it only leads to harm.   Psalm 37:8 (*The Living Bible*)

He who is slow to anger is better than the mighty; and he
that ruleth his spirit than he that taketh a city.
                                        Proverbs 16:32

A stone is heavy, and the sand weighty; but a fool's wrath
is heavier than them both. Wrath is cruel, and anger is
outrageous; but who is able to stand before envy?
                                        Proverbs 27:3, 4

I will therefore that men pray every where, lifting up holy
hands, without wrath and doubting.   1 Timothy 2:8

But isn't there some "righteous indignation"? Yes, there
is. But the Bible makes some very clear distinctions between
our carnal hostility and righteous indignation. I used to
have my own simple formulae. If someone was angry with
me — that was carnal hostility. If I was angry with someone
else — that was righteous indignation! But I'm afraid that
that theology was very poor.

We can discriminate between our own hostile human
feelings and a divine displeasure by using God as our pattern. *God's anger is always directed toward sin and results
from His holy nature.* Psalm 7:11 says, "God judgeth the
righteous, and God is angry with the wicked every day."
*In contrast to this, our anger is usually directed toward any-
thing that gets in our way or frustrates our desires.*

God's anger also coexists with love. He really desires the
best for the unsaved sinner whose sins He hates. Listen to
this verse:

Although God gives him grief, yet he will show compassion,
too, according to the greatness of his lovingkindness. For
he does not enjoy afflicting men and causing sorrow.
                    Lamentations 3:32, 33 (*The Living Bible*)

How different we are. When we resent someone, we usually hope he will get what's coming to him. We hope he

will be hurt or have a difficult time so we can get even. That is not holy anger.

Anger is also sin when we use it to gain vengeance. The Bible says,

> Recompense to no man evil for evil. Provide things honest in the sight of all men. If it be possible, as much as lieth in you, live peaceably with all men. Dearly beloved, *avenge not yourselves, but rather give place unto wrath: for it is written, Vengeance is mine; I will repay, saith the Lord.* Therefore if thine enemy hunger, feed him; if he thirst, give him drink: for in so doing thou shalt heap coals of fire on his head. Be not overcome of evil, but overcome evil with good. Romans 12:17-21

In other words, we are not to try to get even with those who upset us. Let's say your child embarrasses you by throwing a tantrum in the supermarket. This makes you look bad and arouses your anger. To get even, you spank him soundly. This is sin, because you are trying to get even.

Anger is also sin when we use it to protect our self-esteem. When someone says, "Look how those children are acting. I wonder what's wrong with their parents," we immediately come to our own defense. We become angry with our children because they are making *us* look bad. Our anger is a way of saying, "This is *your* fault. Don't you feel ashamed? *Don't try to make me look bad again!*" But this is not good. God wants us to feel good about ourselves, but not at the expense of others. Psalm 89:18 says, "For the Lord is our defence; and the Holy One of Israel is our king." And in a similar vein, Psalm 59:17 reads, "Unto thee, O my strength, will I sing: for God is my defence and the God of my mercy." In Matthew 5:39 we are told to turn the other cheek. [1] We are to do this psychologically as well. When a husband, wife, friend, foe, or child attacks our self-esteem, we should not

---

[1] Matthew 5:39, "But I say unto you, That ye resist not evil: but whosoever shall smite thee on thy right cheek, turn to him the other also."

attempt to even the score or defend ourselves. When we are really confident and trust the Lord for our status, we no longer need the harmful emotion of anger.

A proper form of anger (righteous indignation) focuses on the negative result of sin. Sometimes a misdeed has hurt our child or someone else. We should be bothered by the bad effects of sin. And we are to be angry at the act of sin or at Satan, the author of sin. But we are never to be angry with our children.

Now that we have several distinctions between carnal hostility and righteous indignation, let's summarize their differences in the following table.

Table 3

RIGHTEOUS INDIGNATION AND CARNAL HOSTILITY

	Righteous Indignation	Carnal Hostility	Biblical References
Direction	Toward sin or toward a non-Christian but never toward a son (Christian)	Toward anything or anybody that upsets us	Ps. 7:11 Gal. 5:19-21
Purpose	To right a wrong (or) To promote holiness	To gain revenge (or) To protect self-image	Rom. 12:17-21
Attitude	Exists with love	Exists alone	1 Cor. 13:4-7 Lam. 3:33
Method	Slow and controlled	Rapid and impulsive	James 1:19-21 Prov. 16:32
Result in Child	Increased respect for the parent	Increased hostility toward the parent	Prov. 15:1 Eph. 6:4
Result in Parent	Satisfaction for Christian concern	Relief from expressing hostility, followed by guilt over losing temper	

Seeing the differences between carnal hostility and righteous indignation is the starting point for resolving hostile feelings. By getting the biblical viewpoint on anger, we soon realize that most of our hostility is the carnal kind. Only rarely are we angry with sin in an unselfish, God-like way.

We also need to distinguish between an impulse to anger, which is a temptation, and the harboring of that anger or directing it toward another person. Ephesians 4:26 says, "If you are angry, don't sin by nursing your grudge. Don't let the sun go down with you still angry — get over it quickly" (*The Living Bible*). At first glance this passage seems to be saying that it is all right to be angry for a few hours or to lose our tempers and get it over with. But this interpretation would conflict with the many clear passages where anger is declared to be a sinful emotion. James 1:14, 15 resolves this seeming conflict. That passage reads, "But every man is tempted, when he is drawn away of his own lust, and enticed. Then when lust hath conceived, it bringeth forth sin: and sin, when it is finished, bringeth forth death." The initial lust (in this case the first impulse to anger) is temptation, not sin. But if we allow that temptation to be conceived, it becomes sin. Anger is conceived the minute it is directed toward another person. Combining these verses with the previous passages we get the following picture.

1. The initial impulse to anger is temptation, not sin. James 1:14
2. If that first impulse is nursed or conceived it becomes a sin. James 1:14; Ephesians 4:26.
3. There are several tests to tell us when that initial impulse has turned to sin. These tests are its direction, its purpose, its attitude, its method, its results in the child and its result in our lives. (See table 3 on page 140.)

Let's say your child breaks a favorite vase. Your first response may well be an impulse to anger. That first feeling is not sin. It is temptation. But the moment you direct any of that anger toward your child or harbor it in your mind, that impulse has been conceived. We should recognize that first impulse and refuse to let it develop into sin by directing it toward another person.

This concept may be difficult for us to accept. Since we have all experienced emotions of anger throughout our lives, we find it hard to believe this biblical teaching. We begin to rationalize by saying, "Anger is okay if it is controlled"; "My anger is righteous indignation"; "It's all right as long as I get it out of my system and don't harbor it for long"; "If my child doesn't learn to accept my anger, he will be unable to cope with it in the outside world." We think, "We must teach him the realities of life." But all of these rationalizations pale beside the clear biblical teachings on this emotion.

Psychological insight explains why the Bible so strongly exhorts us to "put away wrath." There are only three possible reactions to anger. These are fear, shame, and hostility. Each of these are damaging emotions. In giving vent to our anger, we invariably instill one or more of these negative feelings. Surely we should try at all costs to avoid creating anger and fearful emotions in our children. Perhaps we should say a word about shame since some may initially see this as a good result. Shame is a feeling of being a bad or unworthy person. It is experienced as an attack on our self-esteem and causes feeling of depression. It should not be confused with a sense of conviction over wrongdoing. Conviction for misdeeds is healthy and desirable. The difference is this. Conviction comes from a loving awareness of misdeeds and results in a desire to change. Shame arises when correction is associated with anger and it results in feelings of depression.

The next step in resolving anger is learning to place our feelings in a biblical perspective. First Thessalonians 5:18

says, "In every thing give thanks: for this is the will of God in Christ Jesus concerning you." The apostle Paul repeats this command in several other New Testament passages:

> Giving thanks always for all things unto God and the Father in the name of our Lord Jesus Christ.   Ephesians 5:20

> Be careful for nothing; but in every thing by prayer and supplication with thanksgiving let your requests be made known unto God.   Philippians 4:6

> And whatsoever ye do in word or deed, do all in the name of the Lord Jesus, giving thanks to God and the Father by him.   Colossians 3:17

These verses are saying that a Christian shouldn't get pushed out of shape when things don't go his way. *A Christian never needs to lose his cool.* We must remember that God screens every event that comes into our lives. There are no "accidents" with God. This gives a new perspective. Instead of becoming angry when things go wrong, we look for lessons to learn. Romans 8:28, 29 elaborates on this principle: "We know that in everything God works for good with those who love him, who are called according to his purpose. For those whom he foreknew he also predestined *to be conformed to the image of his Son,* in order that he might be the first-born among many brethren" (RSV).

God's primary purpose in our life is to conform us to the image of Christ. He wants to mature us and develop the positive fruits of the Spirit.[2] But how does this come about? Not by chance, I assure you! It takes pressure, discipline, and hardship. Just as your child grows by not having his every whim, we grow through frustrations that enter our lives. Not every experience in life is good. *But every experience works for good* when we are willing to grow through it and develop a more Christ-like character.

---

[2] Galatians 5:22, 23, "But the fruit of the Spirit is love, joy, peace, long-suffering, gentleness, goodness, meekness, temperance: against such there is no law."

Let's say your child spills milk on a clean table cloth. Your first impulse is anger. "What's the matter with you!" you might have exclaimed. "You know better than that!" But wait a minute. The Bible says anger is sin. We are told to give thanks in everything. How do we apply these verses to this very practical family problem?

We should begin by asking, "What could God possibly want me to learn from spilled milk? Could it be patience? Or maybe greater respect for my child?" Maybe He just wants to help you have a quiet, peaceful meal! In any case, *you begin by focusing on your problem,* not your child's! This is the only way to resolve anger. By focusing on your child, your mate, or the situation, you will become angry and start blaming others. Only when you look at yourself can you change your hostile feelings.

The next step is to say, "Thank You, Lord, that my son spilled milk so You could teach me a lesson." Now you may not want to learn a lesson this way! If so, be honest. Tell God you don't want to learn, and go ahead with your chaotic mealtimes. We should never deny our honest emotions. Only as we are free to accept our negative feelings and discuss them can they really be resolved. We usually go to one of two extremes. Some of us routinely take out our anger on others with no attempt at change. Others of us try to deny negative feelings to protect our self-esteem. Neither of these will solve the problem. We need to feel good enough about ourselves to admit to negative feelings and seek to resolve them. Once you are committed to let God help you through your frustrations, an interesting thing happens. As you thank God for hard times, you begin to see daily frustrations as God's vehicles for developing your character. Spilled milk is no longer a cause for anger. It is a time for rejoicing! It is an opportunity to grow!

But what about your child? When you stop losing your

temper, won't he start acting worse? *Not at all.* He will begin to improve, since parental hostility stirs up more anger in
your child. Proverbs 15:1 says, "A soft answer turneth away
wrath: but grievous words stir up anger." As a matter of fact,
it is only after your anger is resolved that you can discipline
properly. When you have genuinely thanked the Lord for
spilled milk you can calmly decide how best to discipline
your child. You may realize it was an accident and say sym-
pathetically, "That's too bad, Sammy. We all have accidents
sometimes." You may decide to discipline by logical consequences if the milk was spilled on purpose. When a child
can't eat without messing up the table, he should leave the
table. If the spilled milk episode turns into a regular thing,
you may decide to let him eat alone. That will stop his attention-getting behavior! You may also decide to discipline
by spanking. But this would usually be an unwise choice at
mealtime. Spankings generate anxiety and usually only make
things worse.

One person responded to the spilled milk episode by saying, "One may say, 'Thank You, Lord, that my son spilled
milk,' but does one ever say, 'Thank You, Lord, that my
twelve-year-old son just slapped his mother'? It seems to me
that our response *ought* to be one of controlled anger, with a
reasonable and appropriate form of discipline."

This is a natural reaction and has much to commend it.
This man realized that unbridled anger has a negative result.
But since anger is such a common emotion, he had difficulty
believing that it must be sinful. My reaction to his question
about thanking God when a mother had just been slapped
was, "Yes, that's exactly what we should do." Only as we
first see our own needs and resolve our own negative responses can we be truly free to discipline correctly. If we
attempt to discipline before our anger is resolved, we mingle
correction with our ventilation and arouse feelings of anxiety,

shame, or anger in our children. We also need to realize that
any time a child attacks us in this way we have probably
provoked him into anger. Ephesians 6:4 says, "And, ye fathers, provoke not your children to wrath: but bring them up
in the nurture and admonition of the Lord." Physical attacks
on parents are nearly always the result of parental provoca-
tion. If we respond to his anger with more of the same, we
are actually fighting fire with fire. We are saying, "You
shouldn't be angry and hit your mother; so I will be angry
and punish you." In doing this we are actually setting an
example of anger for him to imitate and perpetuating the
power struggle.

The basic point is this. There are many ways to discipline
a child, but none of them can be completely effective until
you have resolved your own frustrations.

There is a side benefit in this for parents. Little frustrations often ruin our days. "Small" irritations gradually add
up to an unhappy life. But God has provided a solution. By
placing even potentially upsetting experiences in the light of
God's sovereign will, we overcome negative emotions. Life
becomes a thrilling experience instead of perpetual frustration. God actually uses our children's misbehaviors to mature
us as much as He uses our discipline to train them. The intimate relations of family living are usually God's best tools
for changing our behavior. Without gradual refinement we
would go to our graves with all our present hang-ups. But
as we face God's plan of growth for our lives, we develop a
new attitude. We want to work out family frustrations for
a threefold purpose. We want to give our children a good
start in life. We want to have harmonious home relations.
And we want to develop Spirit-filled attributes in our personal lives. Overcoming hostility is one of the greatest hur-
dles in this direction.

Chapter 12

GUILT: YOUR CHILD'S BEST WEAPON

I realize that many people are in the process of becoming sensitive to pent-up emotions like hostility and may need to get these feelings out to resolve their inner conflicts. If this is true of you, don't use the concepts of this chapter to repress your anger; go for needed counseling or learn to express your anger in a harmless way with an adult. Don't sacrifice your children's mental health in trying to resolve your own frustrations.

Children have probably evaded more responsibilities and conned parents into more permissive behavior by guilt than by any other method! If our child can only make us feel, "I am being a little cruel"; "Shouldn't I help him more?" or "Maybe it's my fault," he has us where he wants us. He knows we can't maintain our regulations or mature behavior for long if we are suffering from parental guilt. We will have to give in, in time!

Guilt is an emotion associated with badness, sinfulness, or misdeed. It comes when we feel we have done wrong or fallen short of a standard. Guilt is typically used in two different ways. Real guilt results from the conviction of the Holy Spirit when we sin. It is God's way of letting us know when we are wrong. This conviction is obviously a good thing. It is one of God's ways of helping us mature.

False guilt or pseudo guilt is another matter. This feeling doesn't result from the conviction of the Holy Spirit. Instead, it is our own self-inflicted feeling of failure. Conviction comes when we fall short of *God's eternal standards*. False guilt comes when we fall short of our *self-established standards*. This feeling of false guilt is the focus of this chapter. As parents, we often have a feeling of false guilt. This is a negative emotion and one that our children use to manipulate us into treating them differently. If our children convince us we are being unjust, overly firm, or not helpful, we start to feel guilty. This isn't the Holy Spirit convicting. It is our own overdeveloped conscience or undue sense of responsibility.

Sometimes we feel we should do something for our child when he should actually do it for himself. This is a form of false guilt. Other children play on our guilt by saying, "But everyone else does it. Why can't we?" Once again, this can make us feel bad for depriving our children. This is exactly what they want. If they succeed in making us feel guilty, we may let them have their way. In every instance, this form of psuedo guilt is bad. It is frustrating to parents and allows children to shirk their responsibilities.

HOW CHILDREN USE GUILT TO AVOID RESPONSIBILITY FOR SCHOOL WORK

Sharon was a sixth-grade student at the local elementary school. She was a bright girl who did well in her studies. But Sharon was a procrastinator. The morning of her spelling quiz she frantically tried to memorize her list. The day of her music lesson she tried to cover the whole week's work. And the night before a paper was due — well, it was havoc. Sharon would put off a big project for weeks. Then she expected mother and dad to pull her out of the mess. Mr. Sall, her father, was sent downtown for some art supplies while mother and Sharon began writing the report. It was past bedtime, but Sharon said, "*Mother,* I have to get it done if I stay up all night." So they kept working. Sharon would write, mother typed, and dad tried to keep out of the way! Around midnight the report was finished. Everyone breathed a sigh of relief and went to bed. Sharon vowed this would never happen again, but everyone knew better. This was her pattern, and Mr. and Mrs. Sall couldn't change it . . . or could they?

Why did the Salls repeatedly allow Sharon to draw them into this hassle? The answer lies in the Salls' feelings about themselves. Since our image of ourselves as parents is tied up with our children, when they succeed, we feel parental pride. But when our children fail, our egos take a beating. If our children are not working up to potential, we take it personally. We feel we have failed. We feel guilty.

But wait a minute. Whose responsibility is it to do the report on time? Sharon's? Or her parents? By taking responsibility for Sharon's studies, the Salls have caused two problems. They robbed Sharon of an opportunity to learn to accept responsibility and they caused themselves unnecessary work and worry! Scenes like this are all too common. Parents sense an undue responsibility for their children's behavior and the children exploit the parents' weakness by playing on their sympathy. What can be done for problems like this? The answer is simple. Parents must realize the limits of their responsibility and allow children to learn their responsibility through natural and logical consequences.

Tables 4 and 5 picture good and bad distributions of responsibility for school performance.

Table 4

IMPROPER DISTRIBUTION OF RESPONSIBILITY

Parent's Responsibilities	Teacher's Responsibilities	Child's Responsibilities
1. Remind child of his lessons.	1. Force children to do their work.	1. Listen as mother keeps reminding about homework.
2. Ask child if he has done his homework.	2. Keep reminding children of their lessons.	2. Put things off until the last minute so parents will help.
3. Make an extra trip to school or down town because child has failed to do his part.	3. Do the work for the children.	3. Help mother and dad with the lesson.
4. Help child by doing some of his work.	4. Make things easier so children won't have to work so hard.	4. Blame the teacher or parents if he gets a poor grade.
5. Punish or reprimand child for not doing his work.		
6. Feel guilty for child's failures.		

Table 5

PROPER DISTRIBUTION OF RESPONSIBILITY

Parent's Responsibilities	Teacher's Responsibilities	Child's Responsibilities
1. Provide a place to study.	1. Provide stimulating learning environment.	1. Plan his schedule to have sufficient time for study.
2. Provide an atmosphere which encourages growth and learning.	2. Provide learning materials and aids.	2. Keep track of his own assignments.
3. Provide limited instruction occasionally, without taking responsibility from the child or teacher.	3. Provide instruction.	3. Do his own work.
4. Help the child plan a study schedule but then stay out of the nightly coercion routine.		4. Turn papers in on time.
5. Establish logical consequences, then stay out of homework battles so the child will have to learn responsibility.		5. Accept full responsibility for his own grades.

Notice that the parent, teacher, and child all have certain
areas of responsibility. *But they are different.* The teacher's
prime responsibility is to *instruct,* the parent's major responsibility is to *provide,* and the child's responsibility is to *do!*
When parents step into the responsibility of either teacher or
child, they are asking for problems. Their child will start
side-stepping his responsibility, conflicts will begin, and a
feeling of guilt and frustration will rise. This scene is bad for
everyone concerned. The following excerpt from a seminar
in child rearing shows two mothers working through their
feelings of guilt and learning to let children take responsibility for their own school work.

> Betty:
>
> I'd like to say something about this homework bit. Just
> before Easter Bill came home and said he had to have two
> book reports turned in or else he would get a lower grade.
> They were already late, but he said his teacher gave him a
> second chance. I thought, *Well, will he do it?* I didn't say
> anything to him or remind him over Easter. Sure enough,
> when the reports cards came home, he didn't have those
> two book reports and he got a grade lower. I was so sur-
> prised when I saw his report card. He is usually a very
> good student. It really upset me . . . . I didn't cry in front
> of him, but I sure cried later. *I thought it really was my
> fault.* I could have reminded him to put those book reports
> in. But since I had decided to let him learn his own lessons,
> I refrained from reminding him.
>
> Discussion Group Leader:
>
> I think the important thing is your insight into your guilt.
> You feel it's *your* fault if he doesn't get good grades. Guilt
> is probably the biggest thing that keeps us from natural
> consequences. We have an interesting defense mechanism.
> If we nag and say, "You've got to get this report done," and
> he doesn't do it, we don't feel guilty. We think, "I did my
> part. Now it's all his fault." But if we don't nag and the
> grade comes out bad, we feel we didn't do our part. Nag-
> ging is more for our benefit. We feel it helps to discharge

our responsibilities so we won't be guilty. We really don't feel as bad about his failing as we do about our failing. This applies to nearly every area of logical consequences. It is usually our own guilt that keeps us from letting children profit by their own experiences.

Alice:

This was really a week for us! Monday, Susan came home and said, "I have to have a 9"x12" piece of plywood for a felt flower mat to turn in tomorrow." I said, "Did your teacher just assign it today?" She said, "No." I said, "Well, why didn't you tell daddy over the weekend so he could buy it? I guess the only thing you can do is call him at work and see if he has a scrap piece down there." . . . Luckily for her he did. But it didn't get dry and I don't know what kind of a grade she got on it. I have a feeling she didn't brag about it much!

Marilyn:

I had an experience with Brad this week. He rushed through all day Sunday working on all of his presidents' reports. He rushed through too fast to get a good grade on them. But I refused to get excited about that.

Discussion Group Leader:

Did you refuse to get excited or were you excited and refused to say anything about it?

Marilyn:

No, I really changed my attitude. I actually praised the Lord because I could see that it was teaching me patience. These things were getting to me before and it wasn't doing me any good at all. Now I'm not letting them bother me.

You can see how the pattern usually runs.

1. A child fails to take responsibility for his work.
2. A parent sees potential failure and senses a responsibility to avoid the failure. (This is his first mistake.)
3. The parent's guilt over the child's potential failure motivates him to intervene and take over part of the child's responsibility. (His second mistake.)

4. This is what the child wanted (consciously or unconsciously), so he allows the parent to help him out.
5. The parent does some of the work (his third mistake), and both parent and child are happy. The parent has a successful child (he thinks), and the child has someone else do part of his work.

Alice, Betty, and Marilyn were learning to break this pattern by recognizing the limits of their responsibilities and making their children take responsibility for their own successes and failures.

All of this is not to say that we shouldn't help our children with their schoolwork. There are times for advice and guidance. Problems come that children didn't understand at school and mom or dad can help. Young children also need help in planning their study time. If school work is not done, a logical consequence is no television after supper. In times like these, parents have a role. But the older children grow, the less responsibility we should take. Parents may be "experts" or "consultants," but we must never be drawn into a power struggle or fall prey to accepting a child's academic responsibilities.

This all seems fine as long as Johnny is doing well. But what happens when he falls behind? He is probably testing you to see if you will come to his rescue! *Don't do it!* Underachievement in homes of average and above average social status is usually a child's way of manipulating his environment.

There are four main reasons for academic underachievement. Some children are born with *minimal intellectual endowment.* We should naturally expect limited scholastic performance from these children and adjust our goals accordingly. Other children have suffered *"minimal brain damage" and have what educators call "perceptual disturbances"* or *"learning disabilities."* These children often have problems in reading and arithmetic because of the perceptual tasks involved. Some of these children also show unusually high energy levels and poor coordination. This may lead to "hyperactivity" and "behavior disturbances" in the classroom. Although many of these children have average or even superior intelligence, they need special instructional procedures to overcome their learning disabilities. Children with *severe psychological disorders* also function poorly in school. A deeply depressed child, for example, may be almost totally unable to marshall his energies for study. A psychotic child who is out of touch with reality is obviously unable to concentrate on academic chores. *Parental manipulation* is the fourth cause of underachievement. When a child is not of limited intellectual ability, is not suffering from a perceptual problem, and is not severely emotionally disturbed, his underachievement is always from poor motivation or parental manipulation.

The first three causes of underachievement demand the professional help of physicians, psychologists, or special educators. If your child has one of these problems, you should get professional help for him. To assist your atypical child you may have to use procedures which differ somewhat from those in this book. But if your child is of average intelligence, with no perceptual problem and an essentially normal personality, you must not fall prey to allowing your guilt feelings to make *you* assume responsibility for *his* work.

Underachievement in "normal" children always reflects a child's attempt to gain power, manipulate, or get revenge on parents. A good way for children to express anger toward parents is to do poorly in school. The stronger the parents' need to have an achieving child, the greater the opportunity for revenge. When we scold, nag, coerce, or punish, we actually reinforce their underachievement. The child gets added attention as well as the satisfaction of knowing he is upsetting us.

The only way to resolve this problem is to step out of the struggle. We must resolve our own guilt and say, "My child's school performance is up to him. I will provide a stimulating environment, a place to study, and occasional help. But if my child refuses to take responsibility for his behavior, he must suffer the consequences. When we reach this place (not an easy task!), an interesting thing occurs. Our children soon begin to improve.

Harvey was fourteen years old and had been bringing home "D-" grades for years. His parents nagged and warned that he couldn't get into college and would therefore be a failure in life. They tried frightening him into better grades, shaming him into better grades, and bribing him into better grades — all to no avail. When they learned the idea of limited parental responsibility and natural consequences, they decided to lay off. They told Harvey, "We are sorry we have been bugging you about your grades. School is really your responsibility. If you want to do better, that's fine, but if you choose to get 'D's' that's okay with us." Next term Harvey had all "C's"! What happened? Harvey was unconsciously getting poor grades to punish his parents. When they overcame their guilt and refused to be hurt by his "D's," Harvey had no more reason to underachieve. As a matter of fact, it was rather unpleasant because he really wanted to be accepted by the kids at school and by his teachers. Until his parents changed, however, Harvey was willing to suffer the consequences of poor grades for the privilege of hurting his parents!

Guilt makes parents deprive children of responsibility and keeps them at immature levels of development. It is destructive to the parents' mental health and leads to inadequate child-rearing methods.

CRYING: ANOTHER WAY TO MANIPULATE PARENTS THROUGH GUILT

Guilt causes some parents to refuse to spank their children. Jim Jordan was this type of father. As a child, he had been beaten mercilessly by his dad. He hated his father for it and vowed never to treat his children that way. When his children started to misbehave, Jim had a problem. He knew they needed discipline but he couldn't spank them because of his own guilt. He tried to reason with them and this sometimes worked. But it wasn't long before his children learned that their dad wouldn't enforce limits and began to develop further unwanted behavior. Because of his guilt, Jim lost control of his children.

How do you feel when your child cries deeply? You have just spanked him and he is in great pain. He gets that pitiful look in his eyes, and it tears your heart out. You feel wretched! You actually hurt that poor little child! If your feelings are deep enough, you hug your child and say you're sorry. Or you may not spank him again because you felt so bad. What has happened? Your child has manipulated you into treating him permissively by playing on your false feelings of guilt.

Emotions like this also cause marital conflicts. When a husband believes in physical spankings, and the wife does not, serious arguments arise. "You are so harsh!" Mrs. Abbot sobbed. "I may be harsh," her husband adamantly replied, "but these children are going to learn to respect authority!" Both parents are upset and the child is caught in the middle. In problems like this, the truth usually lies somewhere in between. The one parent is afraid to use physical discipline at all, while the other is harsh and punitive. It takes improved marital communication to resolve this type of problem.

SUMMARY

How can parents get out of the trap of guilt motivation? We have looked at several principles which can guide us. *The first step is to recognize the child's sphere of responsibility.* When this is done, we need not feel guilty for his misdeeds. *The second step is to look at our sphere of responsibility.* Here we can err in two ways. We can take on too much, thus depriving the child of his chance to learn responsibility. Or we can take too little responsibility (in discipline, for example) and thus deprive the child of a chance to profit from the experience of his elders or from the lessons of life.

In summary, let's look again at the division of responsibilities. Parents are to train (Proverbs 22:6), discipline and admonish (Ephesians 6:4, Proverbs 23:13), instruct (Proverbs 4:1, 2), love (Proverbs 3:11, 12), and provide for (1 Timothy 5:8). Parents are not to nag, coerce, threaten, or do the child's work. Children are to obey, honor (Ephesians 6:1, 2), and do (Proverbs 20:11). Only as we allow children to make mistakes can they learn to accept responsibility for their actions. Only as we resolve our false feelings of guilt are we able to release our pressure and let children learn for themselves.

Chapter 13

FEAR: THE ENEMY OF
PEACEFUL PARENTHOOD

"But what if he doesn't eat enough?" Mrs. Stewart asked anxiously during a discussion of natural consequences. "Yes," Mrs. Thompson chimed in. "Children need a balanced diet. If I don't force my daughter, she won't eat a thing."

These comments were made by anxious mothers. Parental fears leave parents tense and worried and often cause us to overprotect our children. Under the guise of "concern," we shield our children from the lessons of life.

We have seen that strong feelings cause parents to misbehave. When we are motivated by anger, we sometimes shout or spank our children needlessly. When we are trapped into false feelings of guilt, we may fail to discipline our children properly. When we become afraid, we are also likely to treat our children improperly. Instead of letting children assume responsibility for their own actions, we are tempted to intervene to "protect" them. We don't want to see them hurt, so we step in where we don't belong. Every time this happens we deprive children of their responsibility by sheltering them from natural consequences. This promotes an unhealthy dependency on parents and stifles emotional maturity.

Take eating, for example. In chapter five we discussed this problem thoroughly. But many of us are afraid to apply natural consequences to undereating. We "know" intellectually that nature can handle the eating problem. God created us so that after prolonged deprivation our stomachs get a "hollow" feeling. This is nature's signal to eat. And it is a good one. It requires no nagging, no coercion, and no bribing. But our fearful emotions sometimes override our intelligence. Even though we know children will eventually eat, something wells up inside and says, "Help him! Nag him! Encourage him! He may not eat enough!"

We do the same thing with sibling conflicts, "appropriate" dressing, toilet training, and many other issues. Instead of allowing children to assume responsibility for their behavior, we intervene. Our intervention usually starts a power struggle, upsets everyone involved, and deprives our children of a lesson in responsibility.

WHEN CHILDREN FIGHT

Fighting is an excellent way for children to worry parents. One child, usually the boy, or the older one, "picks" on his little sibling. Soon the innocent victim comes running to his mother, crying, "He hit me! He hit me!" Our initial reaction is toward the older child. We shout, "Bert, I told you to cut that out. Stop picking on your sister!" Bert yells back, "She started it. She hit me first!" "I didn't either," Marsha defends. "He started it." And on it goes. We usually end this scene by telling the older child to stop hitting the little one, instructing the little one to stop pestering the big one, or warning them both to stay out of trouble. Scenes like this are common. And there is usually no way to tell "who started it." It seems as though we are always refereeing some fight, arbitrating a dispute over a valuable possession, or intervening on behalf of an "innocent victim." Sibling quarrels are often the biggest source of parental headaches. We long for peace and quiet and a little "brotherly love."

Let's analyze this common problem. Why is it that children fight and squabble? Going back to the eight major childish motivations, we can begin to understand these fights. In doing battle with a sibling, a child is usually trying to gain power, find parental attention, or get revenge. Given one of these three causes, let's look at what happens when parents intervene in a childish squabble.

One obvious result is increased attention. Every time we intervene, we give our children more attention. This attention is a social reward. It makes it more likely that our children will fight again when they desire our attention!

When we side with one child, we reward his search for power. Whether he was innocent or not makes no difference. The moment we blame one child for a conflict, the other one thinks, "Oh, boy! I'm in control. By crying to mother, I got her to punish my big brother!" Since the "innocent" child's drive for power was rewarded, she will more likely start a fight again. She has learned that this is a good way to control her family!

When a child is blamed for a fight, he becomes angry. If he was guilty, he is angry for being caught. If he was innocent, he is angry because he is falsely accused. In either case, *he wants to get revenge.* One of the best ways to get revenge on a sibling is to fight. Therefore, the older child is likely to start another row to get revenge on his "innocent" sibling!

This analysis shows an interesting fact. We really can't solve our children's squabbles by intervening. No matter whom we blame or how we do it, one of the children is rewarded for misbehavior. This increases the likelihood of another fight at a later date.

The best way to solve these sibling conflicts is to let the children battle it out themselves. But this isn't easy. Here is where our anxieties enter in. We are afraid one child may get hurt. We intervene to protect the "innocent party." This intervention is based on two false premises. The first false idea is that one child is innocent. The seemingly quiet, weak, innocent child has often provoked the other in a subtle way. During a parents' seminar, the mother of a thirteen-year-old boy and a ten-year-old girl asked if I thought her son might be seeking attention by continually picking on his sister. "Definitely," I replied. "But I also wonder what your girl is doing to provoke him." "Oh, nothing," she replied. "Katie is an angel." Finding it hard to believe that any ten-year-old could be an angel, I replied, "Aw, come on. She can't be all that perfect!" "No," she said. "She really is. She will be sitting right next to me on the couch, and Vernon will come up and hit her for no reason." Seeing "innocent" Katie's strategy for attention, I replied, "Why is your daughter sitting next to you?" She said, "Because we are very close." Then it clicked. There was dead silence in the room. Finally she said, "I see it now. Vernon's feeling left out and needs attention. Katie gets it by being good; so he has to get it by being bad."

The same mother soon began to see through more of her daughter's "innocent" behavior. When Vernon upset their mother, Katie would say, "Oh, leave mother alone. You're such a stupid kid. Can't you see you're upsetting her?" The mother later told me, "She was tricking everyone because she was always sticking up for me. I used to think, 'Isn't she a good girl? It's too bad Vernon can't be that way!' Now I see she was doing exactly what would antagonize a thirteen-year-old. Who needs a ten-year-old sister telling him what to do?"

This family conflict shows how hard it is to find the guilty person. It takes two to tango. If one child were really innocent, there would rarely be a childish squabble.

There is another false idea that causes anxious parents to intervene in their children's fights. *This is the belief that a smaller child is weak and may get hurt.* Our children rarely want to hurt each other. When no adults are around, they usually get along. Have you ever observed your children when they didn't realize you were there? They were probably playing well and cooperating freely. But the minute they discovered mom and dad were around, the struggle began. The reason for this is their desire for attention. When children are alone, they have no parent to vie for attention.

And they have no one to intervene. This means they must get their attention from each other and settle their own squabbles. This is usually what happens when parents refuse to intervene. The children learn to meet each other's needs. They seem to decide, "Since we can't get attention from mom and dad by fighting, we may as well give each other some good attention." They also seem to reason, "Since mom or dad won't step in and settle our conflicts, I guess we should work them out ourselves." By removing ourselves from the power struggle of settling our children's quarrels, we can help children learn to get attention in positive ways by living peaceably with their siblings. This doesn't mean we never instruct our children. There are times for us to teach children how to get along with others. But after they understand, we should usually let children settle things themselves. The time for instruction is generally before or after a conflict when emotions are at a reasonable level.

But back to the idea of being weak. We usually underestimate our younger children and our daughters. Even very young children have their weapons! They soon learn to take care of themselves. I had a good experience with this when our son was four years old and our daughter eighteen months.

Debbie was in her playpen in the front yard while I was weeding. Dickie came along and grabbed the beads she was playing with. This sent Debbie into tears which made Dickie angry that she "ratted on him." He picked up my garden shovel (which had a five-foot handle) and whispered to Debbie, "I'm going to hit you." Then he headed toward her playpen with shovel in hand. My immediate impulse was to intervene. But I knew normal children wouldn't purposely inflict severe harm on others. I also knew Dickie was trying to get a rise out of me. He purposely threatened Debbie within my hearing. If he really wanted to clobber her with a shovel, he wouldn't have let me know about it! I kept on working as if I hadn't heard a word, but I slyly kept one eye on Dickie. I didn't trust him completely, and a garden shovel could open a big gash on my little girl's pretty head! Dickie advanced slowly. He raised the shovel over Debbie's head and said again, "I'm going to hit you." About this time I was getting worried! But I forced myself to stay out of their fight. Finally Dickie lowered the shovel and *very* gently touched Debbie on the head. I breathed a sigh of relief. Then little Debbie hit Dickie in the face! That ended it all. Dickie proved he really didn't want to injure his sister. He was just trying to draw my attention in a negative way. Debbie proved beyond all doubt she could take care of herself.

Whenever children try to draw us into their fights by crying or yelling, we need to be very careful. In nearly every instance they are trying to bring us into a power struggle or get us to solve their problems. We should do neither. After a child is a year or so of age, he can usually hold his own, even with siblings several years older. This doesn't mean the older ones couldn't hurt the younger if they really wanted. But they actually don't. Unless they are severely emotionally disturbed, children don't want to injure others. They do want to cause some pain, and they do want to draw our parental attention, but they don't want to do real damage.

We must learn to let our children suffer physically at each other's expense if they are to develop well emotionally. We all want our children to be loving and sympathetic. We think one way to teach this is to spank a child who hurts a brother or sister. Then we force him to say, "I'm sorry." This may evoke the right words, but a spanking never made a child feel sorry for hurting a sibling! He may feel sorry for the spanking, or sorry he got caught, but he isn't sorry he hurt her. *Genuine sympathy never comes through parental pressure.* It comes in only two ways. *It comes through example and it comes through experience.* As we are sympathetic and loving, our children imitate our behavior. This is the best way to teach brotherly love. Children also learn through experience. To learn true sympathy it is necessary for a child to actually hurt another, see him in pain, and regret his actions. I have seen this in our own children. When we told Dickie to say, "I'm sorry," he merely said the words. He felt no sympathy. But when we have refrained from intervening, and he hurt his sister, I have heard Dickie say, "I'm sorry," and have seen him take her in his arms and kiss her. This is true brotherly love and can be learned only when we stay out of children's fights.

One other principle can help minimize our parental anxieties. All children will suffer some physical hurts. This is a part of life. If we are overprotective, we may prevent some temporary physical pain. But we also rob our children of the opportunity to resolve their own conflicts. When they grow up, mother and father can't protect them from the hardships of life. Therefore, we need to be willing to let our children suffer temporary physical pain to learn some lasting emotional maturity.

Chapter 14

BECOMING A BETTER PARENT

After the birth of our first child, most of us realize we aren't totally prepared for the task of parenthood. Coping with children is a big task. It taxes our knowledge of child psychology, tests our patience, and confronts us with many of our own hang-ups. A mother told me recently, "I vowed for years I would never treat my kids the way my parents treated me. Yet I'm always saying something and thinking later, *That's exactly what my mother would say.*" Most of us have had this experience. We want to do what's right, but find ourselves trapped in deeply ingrained, parental habits. These habits can be changed, but it takes some concrete efforts.

A PROGRAM FOR PARENTS

No one learns to be an effective parent overnight. Being a parent is a long-term educational experience. As long as we have children, we can continue to grow. But there is also an important place for a concentrated effort to develop our parental skills. We can improve our family relations in a few weeks or months if we are willing to invest the time and effort. We will all continue to learn, but a short-term, concentrated effort can get us off to a good start.

The normal reader reaction to a new book goes something like this. We read it, get some good ideas, try a few that work and some that don't, and continue on about the way we did before. Sometimes we improve our actions and are encouraged. Other times we fail and feel guilty, since we are more aware of our mistakes. This doesn't need to happen. *If we are willing to invest the time, we can make radical changes in our home environment.*

To help you get beyond merely reading a book a parents' manual has been developed. This manual, *A Guide to Child Rearing,* is coordinated with *Help! I'm a Parent!* It summarizes each chapter and gives practical exercises which help you apply new child-rearing methods. The parents' manual is really the key to this book. It will help you take theory and ideas and turn them into effective means of training your children. The manual is designed for individual use but can also serve as a workbook for a parents' study group or an adult Sunday school class in parent-child relations. [1]

THREE BOOKS EVERY PARENT SHOULD READ

Parents are busy people. Some books on child rearing close with a long list of readings on all aspects of child training. Few of us take the time to read them. In the hope of encouraging your growth, I am suggesting just three books every parent should read. These books are short, readable, and practical. I do not agree with all they say. Parts of some are contradictory to biblical principles. But their value far outweighs their weaknesses. Here is a short critique of each. Taken together, these books cover three important areas in great depth. They discuss in detail the topics of communication, logical consequences, and sex education.

---

[1] A set of lectures and parent discussions by the author are available on cassette tapes. These are designed for both individual and group use and can be obtained by writing the author at 1409 N. Walnut Grove, Rosemead, California 91770.

Between Parent and Child, Haim Ginott, New York: Avon, 1965.

This best-selling book is the finest available on communicating with children. Dr. Ginott gives practical suggestions often illustrated in a humorous way. However, I find one drawback which is common to most secular books. In emphasizing the worth of children and mutual self-respect there is an underemphasis on discipline. Dr. Ginott indicates that physical spanking is unhealthy and reflects the parents' own hangups. This is often true. On the other hand, the Bible clearly indicates a need for discipline, including physical spanking. When read with a critical eye on the lack of emphasis on parental discipline, this book is terrific!

Logical Consequences: A New Approach to Discipline, Dreikurs and Grey, Hawthorne, 1968.

I believe this is Dr. Dreikurs' best presentation of natural and logical consequences. It is filled with concrete examples applying logical consequences to dozens of family frustrations. The major weakness is this: In attempting to emphasize respect of children, Dreikurs advocates family "democracy." He does this in reaction to past authoritarianism which often squelched children or led to rebellion. His criticisms of authoritarianism are often accurate. The solution of "democracy," however, is unsound. Children are not basically good, and God doesn't advocate a family democracy. Children need adult leadership and discipline. The healthy family is based on God-given authority which is exercised in a fair and loving way. This type of authority respects children's opinions but also allows for needed guidance and discipline. In spite of its "democratic" bias, this is still one of the best books available.

How to Tell Your Children About Sex, Clyde M. Narramore, Zondervan, 1958.

Written from a Christian point of view, this is a book for
modern parents. Although we have thrown off many of our
inhibitions and anxieties about sex, it is still a delicate subject for parents. Dr. Narramore gives practical suggestions
on topics such as "When Should Sex Education Begin?"
"Family Dressing and Undressing"; "Curiosity"; "Experimen-
tation"; "Masturbation" and "Bad Language." This book is
especially helpful because it deals with sexual attitudes and
does not merely give information.

SEEKING PROFESSIONAL HELP

Many of us have long-standing habit patterns which resist
our best efforts to change. When this is the case, we should
be willing to seek professional guidance. In the past, psychological counseling had a certain social stigma. There was
the implication that a person "must be nuts to go to a head
shrinker!" But this idea is gradually vanishing. The modern
emphasis of psychology is "community mental health" and
"preventative education." Psychologists are increasingly turning their attention to problems of the "normal" person instead of only the severely disturbed. This is a good trend.

In spite of the decreasing stigma of seeing a psychologist,
many people are still hesitant to seek professional help. They
think, "Maybe it isn't that bad anyway"; "Perhaps it's just a
phase"; "My wife is overly worried," or "We'll let the Lord
handle it." Although there may be some truth to each of
these comments, they usually reflect our efforts to hide our
fear of admitting failure as a parent. Men are more prone to
this than women. Not having to face the daily headaches,
they fail to see the seriousness of some problems. Men also
suffer from a disease known as the "male ego." We don't like
to admit failure. We think, "I don't need any psychologist

to tell me how to raise *my* kids!" Women have it a little easier. They are supposed to be the "weaker sex." They can afford to be "dependent" and ask for advice. But not so with men. We usually put off our "cry for help" until things are really bad or we continue to ignore the problems. After our children are grown, we ask in amazement, "Where did I go wrong?"

As a Christian psychologist, I am greatly concerned that parents seek help early. By nipping problems in the bud, we can avoid years of frustrations and lasting emotional scars. By overruling our ego problem, we can get our children needed help. I should also add this word: Most psychologists view children's problems as family problems. Some parents send their children to a psychologist so that he can solve the problem. This usually does not work. To bring lasting changes, each family member needs to be involved. This doesn't mean we're all emotionally disturbed. It simply means that both parents should be willing to work on their part of the parent-child relationship.

A FINAL WORD

Rearing children is a long task with many ups and downs. Parents of older children often ask, "Is it too late to change?" The answer is no. As long as children are in our home, we maintain an influence. It is true that children are more pliable in the first few years of life. But there is plenty of room for change. By starting now, each of us can work for a gratifying family life. This will pay immediate dividends of increased family harmony. It will pay the long-range reward of a happy, fruitful life for our children. And it will pay the lasting dividend of an eternal relationship with God, the Creator of the universe and of the human personality.

INDEX